Dr. Rita Smith

Empty Nest, Empty Desk, What's Next?

How Boomer Professional Women Are Reinventing Their Retirement

D1564382

outskirts
press

To My Fellow Baby Boomers

TABLE OF CONTENTS

PREFACE

My defining moment arrived, unannounced, on a Sunday afternoon at Philadelphia International Airport. Up to this point, I had been abstractly aware that at some point in time I would retire from my professional career as a human resources executive. After all, I did have a financial plan in place. Over the course of my 30+-year career, my single focus was on achieving success in my field. I earned an MBA and a doctoral degree, worked long hours, created an professional extensive network, received awards, and embarked on numerous business trips across the world. When and how I would make the decision to retire was a murky, fleeting thought. What I would do with my life in retirement did not even register in my consciousness, beyond a brief image of free time and travel.

The clarity and certainty of knowing it was time to retire blindsided me. Ignorance is bliss. Once I made this decision, I thought I was ready to dive into my new life. I had no idea I was headed into deep, turbulent water.

Juggling my ticket, coat, briefcase, carry-on luggage, and iPhone, I collapsed into seat 2D in the first-class cabin. This was my first flight leg to Philadelphia. From there I would connect to Frankfurt, Germany and then onto Bangalore, India. This business trip comprised nineteen hours' flying each way. My Sunday was literally off to a flying start.

Arriving in Philadelphia, I had a couple hours "to kill" in the business-class lounge before my flight to Frankfurt. Knowing that my upcoming airplane meal was a crapshoot, I grazed on the standard lounge fare of questionable cheese cubes, celery sticks, little containers of ranch dressing, and pretzels. At least there was a good Internet connection so that I could "do emails." I opened my computer, noticing a small tremor in my hands. This was a side effect of my 21-day regimen of anti-malaria pills required for the trip to India.

After composing a few emails, I looked up from my computer and glanced around the business-class lounge. By now it was crowded, and electrical outlets for computers and phones were at a premium. The room was full of business travelers, men and women, mesmerized by their technology.

A twenty-something woman interrupted my typing to inquire about an open seat. After a few moments, she shyly asked if the food was free. I responded like a tribal elder and knowingly nodded. Had I ever been that young and green? My mind flashed back to my first global business trip and airport lounge experience. This was over thirty years ago. En route to my first global business meeting, I remember walking into a smoky lounge and a sea of men in business suits. Back then, my own "dress for success" mirrored their male uniform: a dark blue suit of armor--wool jacket with boxy shoulders, a starched white blouse, a ribbon tie, and a wool skirt that fell mid-calf. Fighting the feeling of being an imposter in a costume, I helped myself to the buffet fare and then settled into my leather seat. Here I was, first-generation corporate and a female, sitting in an airline club, holding my Passport and a business class ticket to Europe. Pretty cool.

A loudspeaker page announced boarding for my flight and jarred me back to the present. I packed up my traveling roadshow of matching, designer luggage and headed for the bathroom. As I splashed water on my face, I looked into the mirror and saw a tired, stressed face staring back at me. My mind began racing. At first a whisper, then growing to an internal shout, I heard, " This isn't 'pretty cool' anymore. I'm tired. I'm tired of packing suitcases, eating crappy airport and airline food, being too tired at the end of the day to speak with friends, the incessant buzz of my iPhone email, and putting off the things I enjoy to a nebulous 'someday.' Yes, the money is great and the perks make me feel important. But the scale has tipped. I proved myself in a male workplace. I'm done. I want a life." Where did these heretical thoughts come from? I could hear the creak of Pandora's box opening. So, here in this inauspicious airport bathroom, I first faced the "R" word: retirement.

I had no idea that my decision to retire would evolve in this manner. Having made this decision was a big hurdle. Little did I know that this first hurdle was one of many to come as I stepped into actually *living* my retirement. Again, little did I know that I was not alone in my struggles. Through initially hesitant conversations, in-depth research, and formal interviews, it became clear there is a generation of Baby Boomer women professionals, like myself, struggling to reinvent a retirement that works for trailblazing career women.

INTRODUCTION

Ten Thousand Baby Boomers Retiring Daily

A Bumpy Ride With No Map

As Baby Boomers, we were the biggest generation in America, approximately 78 million strong, until recently eclipsed by the Millennials. Every day, in the United States, approximately 10,000 Baby Boomers (herein referred to as Boomers) retire. We typically leave the workforce with high expectations of long- awaited freedom. Approximately 50% of Boomers retirees leave with a financial retirement plan in place.[1] We leave having received typical retirement gifts-- perhaps a mug stating "I'm Retired: Every Day Is Saturday" or a tee-shirt reading "Retirement: Ready to Rock and Roll" with an accompanying image of a rocking chair and a wheel chair. However, only 5% of us leave the workplace with a life plan for retirement. [2] Another way to view this is that Baby Boomers are facing a major life transition, and over 95% of us have no life plan for this transition. This results in surprising level of dissatisfaction and a lengthy adjustment to retirement. Studies indicate over 54% of retirees report dissatisfaction in years one and two of retirement. [3] On average, it takes approximately eight years for people to report a high level of adjustment to retirement. [4] This is certainly compounded if retirement was involuntary. For Boomer's with professional careers, having invested so much of their time and identity in our work, the shock of retirement is particularly difficult.

For Boomer professional women, those with college educations and careers, this major transition without a life plan is even more difficult. There is no map for our retirement; it is truly uncharted territory. Our parents' retirement model is outdated. Many of our homemaker mothers cannot offer a path. The traditional male model is lacking, as it focuses almost exclusively upon the financial aspects of retirement. [5] While financial planning is critically important, women tend to also put emphasis on the quality of their relationships and life purpose. On average, only 4% of employers offer Boomers education, lifestyle planning resources, or information about encore career opportunities. [6] In addition, Boomer professional women are the first and largest generation of women to define themselves by our work.[7] A retirement model is needed that provides continuity and outlets for our education, productivity, achievements, sense of community, and passion for meaningful work. We do not want to settle into a life stage that relinquishes hard-earned freedom, political clout, and professional identity. Just as decades ago, we were pioneers entering the professional workplace; we are now facing the new frontier of our retirement.

Retirement Ready?

This concept of Boomer professional women facing the challenges of retirement is a personal one for me. After thirty-five years in professional corporate roles, obtaining advanced educational degrees, and advancing up the corporate ladder, I truly looked forward to retirement. I realize the opportunity for higher education and a professional career was not possible for the women of the "Greatest Generation." I am, therefore, grateful for the opportunities.

Like many of my peers, my entrance into the former male bastion of professional careers was fraught with the challenges of being a trailblazer. I found myself emotionally and professionally bushwhacking through an unfamiliar and often hostile territory. My career began in 1980 as I entered this male-oriented workplace. However despite my opportunities, the work world I encountered had women "dressing (like men) for success" with boxy jackets, shapeless long skirts, button-down shirts, and topped off with a ribbon "bow" tie. Out-of-town business trips often involved a visit to an adult entertainment establishment, leaving me to return to the hotel alone. For years, I was the lone female on the leadership team. While employed at a large banking institution, I worked on the 11th floor. The only women's restroom was the public restroom in the lobby. Sexual overtures and innuendo were commonplace. I earned less than my male counterparts. I struggled with the decision of whether to have children. My workaholic behaviors ruined a marriage. There were few women with whom to commiserate or seek support. Given the limited number of opportunities for female professionals, we tended to view each other as competition. Over the years, the working environment did morph into generally a more favorable place for women. For many of the women in Generations X and Millennial, this "feminist struggle" is ancient history. They look incredulously at Boomer women sharing early "war stories." The cost of our trailblazing was high.

Similar to my professional women peers, I did like the financial independence, the stimulation of colleagues, the broadening experience of global travel, and of course, the recognition and rewards for success. Fast forward to 2013, and the climb up the corporate ladder was losing its luster for me. I had "proved" myself. I was more than ready to step out of this lifestyle.

I had a solid financial retirement plan in place and looked forward to freedom, no alarm clocks, and leisure. This was exhilarating for a few months. Then a sense of loss and uncertainty set in. My work friends had moved on. Volunteer opportunities did not leverage my experience or knowledge. After managing a multi-million dollar corporate budget, as a volunteer, I was forced to spend eight hours being trained on how to balance a $100 cash draw for a not-for-profit store. I flitted around, directionless, taking every workshop and certification I could find. In retrospect, education was a familiar safe place where I could accomplish success and receive recognition. After completing a 500-hour hypnotherapy certification program with truly no interest in hanging a hypnotherapist shingle, I knew it was time to look realistically at my life.

Retirement Shock

For me, the retirement I had so looked forward to was not working for me. I was embarrassed to admit my disappointment or share this with others. After all, I was the one with a retirement countdown clock obviously placed on my desk! This unexpected and totally unplanned struggle with my new post-career identity left me dissatisfied. I had no roadmap for this transitional life stage. Desiring to move on from this disappointment, I began researching resources that could help me. Surprisingly, I found very few resources specifically targeting a Boomer professional woman's unique experience with retirement.

I was part of the Boomer women trailblazers, whose historic entrance into the professional workplace was viewed as a breakthrough. Similar to my peers, I experienced high levels of personal sacrifice in an effort to "measure up" to our male counterparts. I joined a generation of Boomer women increasingly defining ourselves by our professional roles. Responsible for a majority of household management, I struggled with the amorphous concept of "work/ life" balance. This left little time to reflect on what makes my soul sing, create a retirement life plan, or engage in activities offering continuity into retirement. This void translates into having no life plan for retirement.

There were general resources available on retirement financial planning and general life planning. However, there resources did not capture the experience or perspective of Boomer professional women facing the unknowns of retirement. Compounding this conspicuous lack of resources, few Boomer professional women openly shared their shock and dissatisfaction with their retirement experience. With trepidation and fortified by consuming two glasses of wine, I shared my experience with a few other Boomer professional women retirees (or soon-to-be retirees). With hushed tones and hesitation, they shared their similar experiences. I remember instantly feeling like I was no longer alone with my "retirement shock" experience. A floodgate burst open as professional Boomer women opened up and began sharing their retirement experiences. What began as serendipitous conversations morphed into my two years of interviewing over 200 Boomer professional women in different phases of retirement. I leveraged my former professional networks and also communicated my desire for interviews via social media. The response was enthusiastic. The women were at different points in their retirement, from pre-retirement to three to four years into this transition. This ethnically diverse group of US women had successful careers in both profit and not-for-profit organizations.

Both Early (born between 1946-1955) and Late Boomers (born between 1956-1964) were represented. The Early Boomer women pioneers drove changes encompassing women's rights, civil rights, abortion, and the changing family structure. Demographically, the Late Boomers leveraged the Early Boomers entry into male institutions and were supported by the changes the Early Boomer women set into motion.[8] There were legal wins, but the pace of real change in the workplace was not always in lockstep. Many of the challenging behaviors just went underground. This resulted in a strong connection between the two Boomer groups in their sacrifices to prove themselves, over-identification with work, and lack of reflective time to create a robust lifestyle retirement plan. Therefore, their overall perspectives regarding retirement had more similarities than differences.

The Interviews

Of the estimated 78 million Boomers living in the United States, approximately 9 million are African-American, and 7 million are Hispanic. My interviews included corresponding percentages of African-American and Hispanic professional women as part of the total group. On many points regarding retirement, the non-white women align with the larger group of white women professionals. However, their perspectives of Boomer childhood and career obstacles are unique relative to white women. Many African-American women experienced childhood prior to the passage of the Fair Housing Act of 1968, prohibiting discrimination concerning the sale, rental, and financing of housing based on race, religion, national origin and sex. Therefore, they do not share the memories or influences of growing up experiencing the "great American dream" of suburbia that characterizes so much of the Baby Boomer experience. Beginning in the 1970s, the Fair Housing Act opened up suburban living to middle-class and wealthy African-Americans. These non-white groups also have unique perspectives on civil rights activism and additional discrimination beyond the widespread gender disparity overall Boomer women experienced. Aspects of their perspectives are incorporated into the stories appearing in this book.

For the interviews, I employed open-ended questions regarding their retirement experience, probed deeper, and then concluded with asking about lessons learned and advice they had for others. The commonality among these women was astounding. They cited the unexpected magnitude of reinventing their post-career identities. They also noted how unprepared they were to meet the challenge of "retirement shock." They reported feeling isolated, with few resources to provide help. Having years of competent and successful performance in their careers, there was common hesitation to share their unpreparedness for retirement and perceived failure. They struggled with and were at a loss for "what next?"

Given their diverse positions on the retirement time continuum, I was able to collect key characteristics and questions surfacing during each time interval. From the experiences of these women, a process began to reveal itself. There were distinct phases of their retirement transition, unique experiences associated with each phase, and best practices for surviving and thriving in each phase.

Purpose of This Book

This book comprises two parts. The first part of this book focuses on the evolving concept of retirement and the unique perspective of Boomer professional women regarding retirement. Our generation of Baby Boomer women has a unique, historic perspective with which we approach retirement. Comprising almost 40% of the nation's population [9], the sheer numbers of Boomers impacted our world. Unlike our parents' generation, we questioned and embraced change throughout our lives. This resulted in the reinvention of every institution we encountered. It follows suit that Boomers, and particularly Boomer women professionals, will reinvent the institution of retirement.

The second part of this book taps into the collectivism of Boomer professional women facing or experiencing retirement. Studies repeatedly show many of us are unprepared for the lifestyle aspects of retirement. Retirement shock ensues, and we experience a surprising dissatisfaction taking take years to work through. Linking and sharing our retirement stories creates community, breaking the isolation of "retirement shock." Documenting our stories shines a light on an issue unique to Boomer professional women. Capturing our lessons learned and best practices creates a practical roadmap to assist through this major life transition.

Through my interviews, an adjustment process theme emerged. There were distinct phases and actions women took to move through the dissatisfaction they experienced with retirement. I translated this into the Reinventing Boomer Retirement Road Map©. Each step incorporates the best-practice tools used by Boomer professional women to reach the satisfaction side of their retirement. These women agreed to allow me to share their stories in hopes of helping others.

The sections of this book are metaphorically titled with rock and roll music song titles. Rock and roll music had a pivotal influence on the Boomer generation and was literally the soundtrack to our coming of age. The beat and lyrics represented a distinct departure from the older generation's easy-listening music. Rock and roll music possessed a distinctive, fast beat, had lyrics that gave voice to the teenage experience, integrated racial groups, and possessed an undercurrent of sexuality and rebellion. Boomers continue to listen to the rock and roll songs of their youth. A few years ago, my husband attended a concert recognizing the 40th year anniversary of the Allman Brothers' association with the Beacon Theater in New York City. The audience was clearly Boomer fans. Against the backdrop of Eric Clapton's unparalleled guitar playing and the Allman Brothers' improvised jamming, my husband smelled the incongruent combination of liniment and pot. This is truly an archetypical comment regarding the enduring union of Boomers and rock and roll.

Finally, this book is designed to support Boomer professional women as we reinvent our retirement. It provides a roadmap and discovery process to powerfully answer "Empty Desk, Empty Nest, What's Next?"

CHAPTER 1

"THE TIMES THEY ARE A-CHANGIN'"

(Bob Dylan)

Uncharted Territory for
Boomer Professional Women

Retirement 20th-Century Style

Boomer professional women's retirement is an evolving concept. In the context of overall retirement, the 20th century actually gave birth to this new life stage. Prior to this time, workers, primarily farmers, worked their land until they could not lift their hoe or herd their livestock. Their Golden Years, the few that remained, centered on living with their children and withdrawing from active life. To better understand traditional, male-oriented retirement, it is valuable to briefly review its history. What are the origins of retirement, and how has it evolved to the present?

The American Industrial Revolution transformed the

daily lives of Americans as much as—and arguably more than—any single event in US history.[12] From the late 18th through the 19th century, major advancements in manufacturing, transportation, technology, metallurgy, and communications created an economic shift from farm to factory. To farmers, mass-production factory jobs offered higher wages and resulted in a higher standard of living than the life of a farmer working in the scorching sun earning low wages. At the same time, mechanization of farming equipment, such as iron plows, threshers, and seed drills, freed up farm labor to move to higher-paying jobs in urban industrial centers.

Advancements were not limited to commercial production and farm equipment. Early 20th-century improvements in sanitation and increased understanding of disease management increased lifespans. Factory workers were living longer. This improving lifespan created growing numbers of older people unable to meet the speed and physical demands of the factory floor. In 1840, fewer than 4% of Americans were sixty years or older.[13] In 2012, 20% of Americans were sixty years or older.[12] Costly mechanized improvements were being undermined by older workers' slowing productivity.[14] When farmers reached old age, work was adjusted for their capabilities and the extended farm family closed the productivity gap. An aging farmer might move from plowing fields to tending the chickens. The farmer was still contributing to the overall productivity. The factory system did not allow for accommodating limitations. Younger, more productive, unemployed workers impatiently waited in the wings.

Social Security: Paid to Stop Working

The question for industrial management became how to remove the obsolete, minimally productive older workers and replace them with younger, more capable labor. Some employers responded with mandatory "retirement" rules. Then the Great Depression created record levels of unemployment and further drove the need to hasten the exit of older workers. The issue of removing older workers from the workplace was heightened even more. Enter the Security Old Age Assistance and Insurance. The first wave of retirement was born! Social Security actually paid older workers to stop working. Well, technically, older workers paid themselves to stop working, via payroll deductions.

The architects of Social Security selected age sixty-five as the age for Social Security retirement benefit eligibility. Despite the persistent myth that Social Security selection of age sixty-five was based on Germany Chancellor Otto von Bismarck's "old-age insurance" instituted in 1889, this is simply untrue.

The actual calculation of this milestone number may evoke images of 1930s actuaries, cigarettes dangling from their mouths, green visors in place, hunched over their "comptometers." This is partially true. From our current perspective of "Big Data" analysis, it is hard to believe that, according to the Social Security Administration, it was not in-depth data analysis selecting the eligible age of sixty-five but was pragmatism, and stemmed from two sources.[15] One was a general observation about prevailing retirement ages in the few private pension systems in existence at the time. Also, the new federal Railroad Retirement System passed by Congress earlier in 1934 also used age sixty-five as its retirement age. Taking these two factors into account, the Social Security planners made a rough judgment that age sixty-five was probably more reasonable than age seventy. This judgment was then confirmed by the actuarial studies. The studies showed that using age sixty-five produced a manageable system that could easily be made self-sustaining with only modest levels of payroll taxation. So these two factors, a kind of pragmatic judgment about prevailing retirement standards and the favorable actuarial outcome of using age sixty-five, combined to be the real basis on which age sixty-five was chosen as the age for retirement under Social Security.[16]

Retirement was now incentivized. Older people could withdraw from paid labor without incurring poverty and complete dependence on their children. Retirees could now sit in their porch rocking chairs with fewer worries. The late 19th and early 20th centuries were a golden era of American health innovation. Breakthroughs like germ theory, antibiotics, and widespread vaccination, as well as major public-health advances in sanitation and regulation, neutralized many long-leading causes of death. [17] The time span from exiting the workplace to exiting life was increasing. In addition, retirees now had more discretionary income to enjoy. For the first time, between 1947 and 1960, a majority of Americans would enjoy something called discretionary income, earnings that were secure and substantial enough to permit them to enter sectors of the marketplace that were once reserved for the affluent.[18] For many retirees, with increased discretionary funds and increased levels of health, the reality of spending their remaining days in a rocking chair was unacceptable. Enter Madison Avenue advertisement executives.

The sustained economic expansion and employment rates from the end of WWII through the early 1970s opened up middle-class access to the warm and sunny climates formerly the exclusive purview of the rich and famous. Advertisers touted active retirement days spent on sunny golf courses, gliding through the water on paddleboats, or enjoying the mental workout of a game of Mahjong. It turned out that retirees could now work at play!

Exclusive retirement communities began springing up in Arizona and Florida. Real estate developer Del Webb's Phoenix area Sun City was built to "create a community exclusively for America's retired citizens (55+ years old) citizens with attractive, modestly-priced homes and the endless facilities for their recreational and creative activity, based on an entirely new perspective toward retirement living...A New Active Way-of-life." [19] Active adult retirement communities like Sun City were completely self-contained communities with their own library, places of worship, stores, dining, hospitals, etc. Many people traded their cars for the preferred choice for daily transportation—golf carts. Retirees, segregated into a completely self-contained community never even had to leave the grounds. The experience of seeing their younger neighbors go to work each morning would fade into the past.

Phoenix's Sun City, "the Original Fun City," attracted 100,000 visitors on its opening day and grew to a community of concentric circle neighborhoods with 28,000 patio homes. The concept of a community lifestyle, exclusive to retirees, maintenance-free and dedicated to active leisure activities was a revolutionary departure from the previous view that retirees literally retreat from life and recede into old age. It was so disruptive an innovation that *TIME* magazine made Del Webb its "Man of the Year" in 1962.

Retirees could trade in their rocking chairs or join "like-minded neighbors" for golf, a swim in an Olympic-sized pool, or a game of horseshoes or shuffleboard. Or if otherwise inclined, they could try their hand at ceramics, stained glass, or perhaps woodcarving. If they were seeking a more mentally challenging activity, there was always "competitive bridge." Of course, they could join a new interest group, the American Association of Retired People, focused on "productive aging." Thus began the great retirement migration to sunny climates and the birth of the "modern, active retiree."

Not For Boomers

A Baby Boomer and former Florida resident I interviewed, living in close proximity to an age-restricted community, viewed these adult retirement communities more like senior "internment camps." She specifically cited the cookie-cutter blandness of the housing, the insular life-style and the lack of generational diversity in the communities. Others interviewed expressed similar perspectives.

I interviewed a 59-year-old female, Lisa*, as she was launching her retirement plan. Our interview took place as she readied herself to leave her position as Chief Financial Officer of a major pharmaceutical company. "After I announced my retirement date, I can't tell you how many people asked if I was moving to a 'nice retirement village' in Florida. I have nothing against Florida living, but I was surprised at the assumption that my retirement equated to a new address in a tropical retirement community. I've visited my in-laws numerous times at their retirement village in the Tampa area. They have a nicely appointed villa. However, once outside their home, it feels like I am an extra in the movie *Cocoon*. Do you remember the sci-fi movie about a group of rest home people rejuvenated by aliens? I know this sounds harsh, but to me, it is sea of white hair with an eerie lack of young people. The lack of diversity seems so constricting. I just can't picture leaving the active pace of my career for thirty years of endless bridge games. I didn't work for thirty-five years to settle for mind-numbing golden years. My husband distances himself from the possibility of this segregated lifestyle by flippantly referring to these age-restricted communities as 'God's Waiting Room.'"

For many retirees, living a "traditional" retirement,

having the time to do everything they ever dreamed about actually falls dramatically short. In 2013, *US News and World Report* revealed that retirees spend over half their leisure time with remote controls at-the-ready and glued to the "tube."[20] The second-largest chunk of new-found leisure time is spent sleeping, followed by reading. Typically, when working, watching television, sleeping, and reading are high on the average adult professional's wish list. The endless horizon of leisure dulls the appeal of these sedentary and isolating activities when we are no longer immersed in the busy vortex of a professional career. Many professional women I interviewed reported that working made Saturday and vacations more meaningful and coveted.

Boomer Longevity Bonus

My research supports numerous surveys indicating professional Boomers are not interested in pursuing "traditional" retirement focused on leisure. In actuality, career women Boomers view their "longevity bonus" as a chance to pursue new interests and reignite old dreams sidelined by careers and raising a family. Age Wave co-founder Maddy Dychtwald, a leading expert on evolving demographic trends, defines the "longevity bonus" as the thirty years added to people's lifespans in the 20th century.[21] These extra years keep increasing, as confirmed by a new report on mortality in the United States from the Centers for Disease Control and Prevention's National Center for Health Statistics. The center has found that life expectancy has reached a record high of 78.8 years. This figure is actually 81.2 years for females.[22]

Although now being surpassed by Generation X and Millennials, Boomer professional women were the most-educated generation in American history. Given our historic educational breakthrough, professional Boomer women typically view themselves as lifelong learners. As such, they are hungry for continued intellectual and intergenerational stimulation. Retired Boomer women professionals will seek continued education for personal growth and to gain knowledge to launch a new career.

Shifting Retirement Trends

Where retirement historically marked the end of work, today many Boomers consider work as part of their retirement life plan. This is a departure from more traditional retirement where between 1994 and 2000, only 10-12% men and 6-8% women retired (recipients of retirement income) aged sixty-five worked for pay. [23] In a 2014 Center for a Secure retirement study, 28% of all middle- income Boomers report working or having worked in their retirement. [24] Although it is tempting to cite the economic recession or lack of adequate retirement savings as the driver for the increase in working retirees, this is actually not the case for a majority of Boomers. In fact, 59% employed retirees report the primary reason they work is for nonfinancial reasons versus the 41% citing financial reasons.[25]

Boomer retirees are seeking a more flexible work schedule with greater balance between work and leisure. In fact, 59% of employed Boomers work part time, 18% freelance, 7% seasonal, 4% other versus 12% full time.[25] Indicative of desired flexibility and balance, only 10% of employed Boomer retirees have management responsibilities versus 25% pre-retirement.[26] For the added flexibility, most Boomers are willing to work for less money in retirement. There is evidence that the growing trend of employed Boomer retirees has many benefits. Compared to their nonworking Boomer retirees, working Boomer retirees cite less stress, greater emotional health, better family relationships, leisure time more fulfilling, and greater connection with current events.[27]

The following two accounts of retired professional Boomer women represent the two primary reasons for retirement employment. In the first account, Sarah*, a former financial services executive, felt increasing dissatisfaction with her corporate work and shared the increasing yearning of the women I interviewed who worked to reinvent their sense of purpose, keep mentally sharp, and remain connected with others. In the second account, Monica* decided to return to work for financial reasons.

Stories of A Working Retirement

#1 Sarah's Story

"I had a good run in the corporate world. My Wharton degree opened a lot of doors for me. I worked my butt off for years. The first couple decades I did really enjoy the work and the rewards. My sixtieth birthday was a turning point. I had broken through the proverbial glass ceiling, climbed the male-built career ladder, and the view ahead was just more of the same. My son was newly married and my nest was, as they say, empty. My husband had retired two years earlier. At first I attributed my growing dissatisfaction with work to middle-aged angst. Or was it the birthday jolt of realizing that more of my life was behind me than in front of me? My work became more and more a rote exercise providing me increasingly less satisfaction. It became obvious to me that I had reached a tipping point in my career. I could and would retire at the end of the year.

"I knew myself well enough to know that I would get bored at home. I wanted to continue to work, but this time it would be something that would make my heart sing and provide more time flexibility. After some soul-searching, I landed on teaching at the college level. With my MBA and work experience, I was qualified and hired as an adjunct finance professor in the undergraduate business administration program. For the past three years, I've taught one class per semester. I take the summer off to travel with my husband. I love the energy of the students and sharing my real-world business experiences with them. I spend about three hours per week in class and about another fifteen hours per week researching and preparing lessons, grading papers, and coaching students. I feel like I still have a professional identity, but I also have time for my yoga, art, friends, and family."

In this second account, Monica's * decision to work is based primarily on financial reasons. While she has a solid retirement savings, she has a ten-year gap before she will reach seventy years old and receive Social Security income. Additional retirement income will preserve a majority of her current retirement savings for the next ten years.

#2 Monica's Story

"As a divorced female I was always diligent about financial planning and savings for my retirement. In my last role, I served thirteen years as a VP Marketing and Communications for a $5 billion corporation. I was getting more and more drained by managing people and the global travel. Frankly, I was feeling really burned out. Working with my financial advisor, we created a plan where I could retire at age sixty. To maximize my Social Security benefits, I planned to file at age seventy. I wanted the decade between retirement and receiving Social Security benefits to include some travel and my painting hobby. I knew that these leisure activities would be costly. I also knew I did not want to put a large dent in my retirement savings over these ten years. You might say my decision to work in my retirement was based on cash flow.

"Since I made this plan prior to my actual retirement, I began to explore what type of work would offer both downshifting and a reasonable income. Working in my professional field made the most sense, but no longer in a corporate environment. I beefed up my networking efforts and made a connection with our city's Chamber of Commerce. There are 50,000 residents in our city and approximately 600 Chamber members. They were looking for someone to work about thirty hours per week as a public relations director. The role was responsible for press releases and marketing of Chamber/community events and also generating awareness to attract increase Chamber membership.

"I landed the job and started about three weeks after my corporate retirement. The philosophy and pace of a not-for-profit organization works well for me. I have a team of one. She divides her time supporting me and managing the Chamber's website. I have flexibility with my work hours and frequently work from home. I do attend Chamber events, but factor this into my overall weekly hours. I report to the President of the Chamber, which rotates with members every two years. I have enormous autonomy. I enjoy being connected into our community.

"I did trade in a six-figure income for a five-figure one. However, my salary covers my basic living expenses and leaves monies left over for my leisure activities. I am at ease knowing that for the interim decade between retirement and Social Security, I will not deplete the security of my retirement savings. Someone recently described me as 'semi-retired.' I'm not sure what this really means. I do know that I retired from my professional career path and using my skillset in an environment much more conducive to what I want at this stage of my life."

New Take On Retirement Communities

Rejecting traditional resort-type retirement communities, Boomers are reshaping the retirement housing market. We are no longer flocking to the senior ghettos of cookie-cutter retirement communities and high-rise condominiums of days past. [28] Instead Boomers are choosing aging in place, new forms of affinity living, or new university-based retirement communities.

Boomers were the first generation to surpass their parents (Silent Generation) in being the healthiest, best-educated, and wealthiest generation in history. According to a McKinsey Global Institute report, Boomers collectively earned $3.7 trillion, more than twice as much as the $1.6 million of the previous Silent Generation at the same age.[29] McKinsey estimates 80% of Boomer income growth is due to factors specific to Boomers (size of Boomer cohort, increases in education, changes in household structures, and women in the workforce). Only 20% of the increase was caused by long-term economic trends, such as productivity and technological changes, not specific to the Boomer generation. [30] In addition, our frugal parents will bequeath Boomers' inheritance wealth totaling $13 trillion. [31] Unfortunately, this is somewhat offset, as we Boomers are also known for our record amount of debt. However, the bottom line is that professional Boomers have money (and lines of credit!) and are willing to spend money on a customized retirement housing experience.

Customized Retirement Housing

Known as the "me" generation, most Boomers value individuality and diversity over similarity. As consumers, we demand variety in just about everything from cars, electronic, clothes, to soft drinks. Boomers are the generation credited with creating twelve different kinds of Coke. It makes sense that Boomers are driving the variety of new options for retirement housing.

One emerging option is affinity living, communities of retirees created around shared hobbies and interests. Many of these communities have healthcare and assisted living facilities to address future needs. Professional Boomers who never had time for their interests or hobbies during their career years are making up for lost time in their affinity communities. For example, amateur astronomers can view the skies with fellow stargazers at the Chiefland Astronomy Village, where each home has a built-in telescope.[32]

Or perhaps the arts are more appealing? Located in Burbank, California, the Burbank Senior Artists Colony targets older Americans who want to paint, write, and act in their retirement years. Their website touts a 141-unit community with a 40-seat performance theater, artist studios and classrooms, a library, and art display galleries.[33]

While affinity communities are homogeneously organized around common interests, residents find the benefits outweigh the lack of diversity. Residents report feeling instantly at home. They feel connected with other residents, and have satisfaction being immersed in their interests.

Other professional Boomers are headed back to re-experience the college campus lifestyle. This time, rather than arriving in a used Chevy Corvair, we are more than likely pulling up in a shiny Mercedes. Instead of Spartan dormitories with milk crate bookcases, seniors live in luxury college-centric housing developments placed nearby or adjacent to major universities. The University of Florida, Duke University, and Stanford are just a few of the estimated 100 university-based retirement communities (UBRCs). Typically these UBRCs are in close proximity to the university, have formal educational programs for the retirees, offer a range of care from independent to assisted living, and usually have a 10-15% base of alumni to further the connection with the University.

This growing trend of UBRCs target retirees seeking intellectual and cultural stimulation and intergenerational contact. Initial studies point to this environment fostering mental agility and a youthful vibrancy. Some believe it is instrumental in staving off dementia.

Still other Boomers reject the traditional Sunbelt retirement exodus and choose to "age in place." The traditional pull of a mild climate and lower cost of living is not a strong enough draw for healthier and wealthier Boomers. In fact, nearly nine in ten Boomers prefer to remain in our current residences as long as possible.[34]

We cite desire for a familiar, heterogeneous, and more vibrant community. Many Boomers also view ourselves as the emotional and social centers of our families and want the space to accommodate family gatherings. We are willing to invest in future upgrades to accommodate our changing physical abilities, such as wheelchair-friendly doors and hallways.

Bucket Lists

One final driver for Boomers' rejection of traditional retirement is the newly popularized "bucket list." The idea of a "bucket list," a list of things to do before you die, was popularized in the 2007 movie *Bucket List,* starring Jack Nicholson and Morgan Freeman. The storyline is about two terminally ill men living out their wish list of things to do before they die. I have no recollection of my parents, the Silent Generation, ever creating a list of adventures and experiences they must accomplish before they die. Having grown up with the Great Depression, this type of thinking was simply an anathema to their values of hard work, savings, and sacrifice. I recall their lukewarm reception when I shared my upcoming trip to Hawaii intended to accomplish my traveling to all fifty states before I die. The trip, inclusive of first-class air tickets and the beachside Ritz Carlton Resort, cost me $12,000. My father shook his head and muttered something about putting that money to better use. I recall telling him, "I want to fill the bucket before I kick the bucket." Fulfilling a bucket list is a natural extension of Boomers and the mass consumption of our childhoods and adulthoods. "We realize having all the best toys isn't key. It's who has the best and most experiences who wins."[35]

This brings us full circle from my being confronted with the "R" —retirement word in Philadelphia Airport to examining traditional retirement to the reinvention of retirement by my fellow Boomers. We are the largest demographic group in history. We have more education, health, and income than previous generations. Our unique place and time in history resulted in a generation that challenges the status quo, thrives on change, and seeks self-fulfillment. Just as we changed every other life stage and institutions we encountered, we are reinventing what it means to retire. Boomer professional women, as a subset of the larger Boomer generation, are on the front lines of this change. Our entrance into the male work world required sacrifice and frequently working twice as hard to earn our way up the male career ladder. Exiting these hard-fought gains is not easy for us. Focusing so heavily on our careers left us with little time to plan the life we want in this next and last phase of our lives. Yes, our retirement is uncharted territory, but as Boomer career women we have a lot of experience as pioneers, successfully navigating the unfamiliar without the benefit of roadmaps.

TAKING TIME TO REFLECT:

1. To what extent do I have professional women "retirement role models"?

2. When I think of retirement, what images come to mind?

3. At this point, how do I picture my day-to-day retirement lifestyle?

"MY GENERATION"

(The Who)

Understanding the Influences That Shaped
the Baby Boomer Generation

BOOM

The years following WWII resulted in an unprecedented number of US births. Similar trends occurred in many of the former WWII ally countries, as well. This spike in birth-rate became known as the "baby boom" and the descriptor stuck. This extraordinarily high rate of births began in 1946, in which more babies were born than ever before, and is viewed as ending in 1964. Over the 18 years comprising the Baby Boom, approximately 77 million babies were born. This equates to over 4 million babies born each year and 10,000 babies born each day. By the end of the birth boom in 1964, Baby Boomers represented over 40% of the US population.[36]

The events and social trends occurring during a

generation's coming of age form the generation's collective personality. These common experiences and unique place in history foster a shared identity and membership among the generation's peers. For the Baby Boom generation, our most formative years were coming of age in the 1960s and 1970s. These two decades are synonymous with years of profound cultural change. [37]

Early Boomers (born 1945-1954) came of age in a period of historic levels of growth and prosperity, social activism, Cold War fears, and an increasingly divisive Vietnam War. The interplay of each created a unique perspective for Early Boomers resulting in changes inherited by their generational cohorts, Late Boomers (born 1955-1964). Early Boomers are characterized by idealism born from the growth and prosperity of the 1950s and 1960s.

The permissive parenting of this Dr. Spock era is credited for creating a generation known for valuing personal freedom and individuality. Paradoxically, idealism and optimism coexisted with the paranoia and fears generated by the Cold War.

Amidst prosperity and consumerism, the specter of mutual nuclear annihilation was ever-present. This left a residue of skepticism in the psyches of Boomers. We questioned humanity's ability to co-exist on this planet. This perceived uncertainty of life drove many of us to search for greater meaning In our lives.

The Late Boomers came of age in the 1970s. The 1970s was a decade when social activism and related legislative changes continued. Cold War fears relaxed as the US and the USSR entered into an era of temporary détente. The Vietnam war was over, albeit being considered a US loss. The growth and prosperity of the earlier decades ended, replaced by economic recession and inflation. Political scandals added to a cultural malaise in the US. The intersection of these forces added a deeper level of cynicism to the Boomer psyche, particularly to the Late Boomers.

Born in an era of tremendous cultural transformation, the one word that aptly describes their experiences and impact is "change." Boomers experienced rapid and often turbulent change and likewise created change in their world. Boomer professional women share this generational identity around change. Even as Boomers age, we remain a generation questioning the status quo and reinventing the world around us. It is a natural extension that Boomer professional women are open to change as we reinvent retirement. What were the specific events that shaped our generation and characterized our drive for change?

Suburbs: The American Dream

The years after World War II saw a massive movement of white Americans to new suburbs. The growth of suburbs resulted from several forces: mass demobilization of troops, favorable government-backed housing loans, mass production of housing and automobiles, a burgeoning economy, and a spike in marriages and births.

The parents of Boomers came of age during the Depression and WWII, two eras known for their uncertainty, sacrifice, and service. They experienced their fathers' losing jobs, being called up on to help support their families, doing without most consumer goods for nearly two decades, immense patriotism as the United States joined the escalating world war, and experienced losing their young men in the forests of Belgium, beaches of Italy, and islands of Asia. In the post- WWII period, they craved security, sought a suburban family lifestyle, celebrated prosperity, and embraced consumerism After sixteen years of economic and wartime strain and sacrifice, people sought the American Dream of home ownership, prosperity, and a growing family. Unfortunately, this American Dream was solely the domain of white Americans.

In response to migration of African-Americans to Northern cities for abundant war production jobs, white Americans fled the cities, initiating "white flight" to the suburbs. Employment and relatively better treatment in the Northern cities influenced African-Americans to settle permanently.

Spurred on by a variety of catalysts, white America, began the massive move to the suburbs. Potential suburban homeowners took advantage of the new, low -interest Veterans Housing Authority loans or 5% down Federal Housing Authority guaranteed loans. Home ownership was no longer the purview of a small percentage of white Americans. Restrictive rental and sales covenants, however, did block most African-Americans from participating in this expansion of home ownership.

Lessons learned from the rapid construction of wartime military housing and facilities were applied to the mass production of suburban homes. The famous Levittown suburban communities are the typical 1950s suburbs. Between 1947 and 1951, over 17,000 new houses were built in Levittown, equating to 15 houses per day. [38] Pre-fabricated housing elements were quickly assembled into a limited number of undifferentiated models. Most houses, approximately 1,000 square feet, had two or three bedrooms, a living room complete with a picture window, and kitchen. Early homes were ranch style, followed by Cape Cods with potential attic bedrooms, and later came the split-level style. The higher-end homes came equipped with a family room and a bonus television set. Spacious front-porches, allowing neighbors to easily connect, were things of the past. Front porches were replaced with backyard patios.

The daily white, middle-class, suburban cadence was highly predictable. Each day the men commuted to their jobs in the city or to the newly sprawling suburban corporate headquarter buildings. At the close of each day, they drove the family car home to the maze of cookie-cutter houses. Women prepared dinners in their modern Petal Pink or Sunbeam Yellow kitchens. Gangs of playing children dotted the manicured lawns and rode their bicycles in the streets.

On any given Sunday, a drive through the suburbs provided a cacophony of lawn mowers and the aroma of burning Kingsford charcoal in backyard grills. The lyrics of the 1967 song "Pleasant Valley Sunday" (recorded by the Monkees), encapsulates the homogenized conformity of suburban life.

While suburban life represented the hopes and dreams of the parents of the Boomer generation, their children eventually rebelled against this lifestyle, which they viewed as an empty wasteland of consumerism and conformity.

Generation Gap

As young Boomer women came of age in the 1960s and 1970s, some of us openly and militantly questioned and rejected the values embodied in our suburban roots. Some of us gravitated to communes, explored altered states of consciousness, experimented with drugs such as LSD and marijuana, engaged in the freedoms of the sexual revolution, wore Army Surplus clothing, and militantly protested the Establishment, all the while "letting our freak flag fly."

Other young Boomer women more moderately questioned the suburban, traditional values espoused by their parents. We may have joined consciousness-raising discussion groups. To the confusion of our parents, we voiced support of Civil Rights and the Women's Movement. Some women flashed peace signs as we joined in anti-war marches. Bell-bottom jeans filled our closets. Beehive hairstyles gave way to long straight hair or Afros.

Regardless of where on the counterculture continuum we reside, the conformity and homogeneity of the suburbs were catalysts for questioning the status quo, rejecting traditional values and lifestyles, and reinventing a future of individuality and choice. Today's Boomer professional women carry this same mindset of questioning and reinvention as we create our retirement life plans.

Spock Babies

Changes in child-rearing practices also contributed to our Boomer generation's collective personality of individuality and added a sense of entitlement as well. After World War II and the explosion of births, children became the center of the family. This central focus on children was more specific than in any previous generation. Pent-up desire for domesticity led to high expectations for successful child-rearing. The Cold War underscored the fragility of life and the need for strong nuclear families. In 1946, the book *The Common Sense Book of Baby and Child Care*, by pediatrician Dr. Benjamin Spock, rocketed to popularity, revolutionizing 20th-century child-rearing. Spock's manual broke with traditional rigid scheduling, corporal punishment, and withholding of affection. As an advocate of Freud's belief that infantile experiences shape the person, Spock emphasized allowing a child to assert his/her individuality. Developmental areas such toilet training, walking, talking, and self-feeding were based on the child's schedule and rather than the parents' schedule. Spock's book was an instant success, selling 500,000 copies in the first six months, and it went on to be the best-selling book of the 20th century in America, aside from the Bible.[39] Boomer infants became known as "Spock babies."

Older generations blamed this "liberal, indulgent" child-rearing as the cause of the Boomer generation's entitlement and strong sense of individuality. Toy manufacturers were not complaining, though. Exposed to a daily average of four hours of television viewing, children were bombarded with toy commercials.[40] Glued to *Miss Francis's Ding Dong School*, the *Mickey Mouse Club*, or *Captain Kangaroo*, children's demand grew for Mr. Potato Heads, Tiny Tears Dolls, Slinkys, Barbie Dolls, Easy Bake Ovens, Play-Doh, and G.I. Joe dolls. Demand translated into purchases. By the 1970s, the average American child had not just one doll, bear, or truck, but well over ninety toys filling the bedroom. [41]

College Bound

Educational institutions expanded to accommodate the record number of Boomer children. Unprecedented numbers of Boomer girls, dressed in crinoline dresses and patent-leather Mary Jane shoes, attended newly constructed suburban elementary schools. As the Baby Boom years continued, so did the need for increased teacher training and construction of new schools. As life around us shifted to accommodate our critical mass, Boomers could feel our power in the numbers that made us special.

Unlike earlier generations, Boomers were no longer required to drop out of school to provide financial support for their families. Boomer adolescents stayed in school. In 1963, the percentage of student's graduating from high school was 76% compared to the average of 39% during the Depression years.[42] Women represented approximately 50% of those receiving high school diplomas during this period, a number that continues to remain stable. College attendance rates also rose, particularly for women. From 1960 to 1970, as Boomers came of age in record numbers, college attendance doubled from 3.5 million to 7.9 million. The proportion of the 18-19-year-old women attending college rose from 12.2% in 1947 to 34.6% in 1970 and 45.8% in 1988. [43] Whether in crowded halls of high schools or in ivy-covered college buildings across America, unprecedented numbers of Boomer youth shared the same space, experiences, and values. As the result of Civil Rights and Title IX (prohibiting discrimination on the basis of sex in educational programs and activities) legislation, there was increasing educational diversity. This resulted in greater awareness of American society's inequalities. It also cross-pollinated cultural elements such as music. A separate youth culture emerged within society. From hairstyles, clothing, music, social consciousness, and sexual mores, to the buttons and bumper stickers they displayed, the Boomer youth culture was a clear departure from their early childhoods of suburban conformity. A Generation Gap followed, as parents were confounded by their offspring's rejection of traditional values, cynicism toward government institutions, expressions of personal freedom, and idealism for social change. The Pill and access to legal abortions provided young women with an option to delay parenthood. The threat of mutual atomic annihilation contributed to a sense of immediacy and living in the moment. This mindset contributed to Boomers being called the "Now Generation." Boomers are viewed as placing high value on freedom of choice. Boomer professional women carry this into our retirement process.

Social Activism

On college campuses, Boomers were empowered by their sheer numbers and diminished parental supervision. Their mindsets expanded through their education and proximity to increased diversity. This resulted in many college students embracing social activism. Protest posters reflected the breadth of social causes. Boomers marched with posters reading: "Give Peace a Chance," "Power to the People," "Hell No, We Won't Go," "Make Love, Not War," "Fight Pollution Not Wars," "Equal Pay for Equal Work," "No Nukes," and "Pro Choice." In addition to educational studies, Boomer women were learning to find our voice against society's ills. Again, there was a continuum of resistance. Some more militant women chained ourselves to college administration buildings, some of us held placards in protest marches, and others more quietly questioned the traditional thinking that threatened to shape our future. To varying degrees, questioning the status quo and pushing for change was assimilated into the DNA of

Boomer professional women. Their experiences of protest and change, in the 1960s and 1970s drives us, 40 + years later, to question traditional retirement models and to seek a new, redefined post-career lifestyle.

Me Generation

With the advent of the 1970s, a more pervasive cynicism gripped Boomers. The Vietnam War remained an American quagmire, the assassinations of the late 1960s left few viable leaders for Boomer youth, Watergate demoralized faith in government, and the economy was stagnant with high levels of inflation. For Boomers coming of age in the 1970s, the emphasis on social activism shifted to a quest for self-enhancement. Energies to change the world were dampened by national and global happenings resulting in increased disillusionment and cynicism. This was the catalyst for Boomers to adopt a new introspection and focus on self-fulfillment. Self-help books rolled off the printing presses, a new magazine, *SELF*, was launched, fashions were outrageous statements of self- expression (think platform shoes and pastel leisure suits), and divorce rates soared. Impacting one's own happiness became key. Boomers, and particularly Late Boomers, were titled the "Me Generation." Self-fulfillment is a key theme as Boomer women professionals frame their retirement years. The "bucket list," a unique Boomer invention, is symbolic of this search for self-actualization and achievement of personal goals.

Small Box, Big Impact: Television

The final two cultural areas influencing the Boomer generation are television and rock and roll music. Beginning in the early 1950s, Americans spent evenings sitting in front of the flickering black and white images of over 6 million television sets. [44] Welcomed into suburban homes were "the Beaver," "Kitten," "Timmy and Lassie," and "Little Ricky." Television depicted the ideal, perfect, white middle-class family: Dad toting his briefcase to work, Mom wearing her pearls to vacuum, and two mischievous but obedient children. The key messages were conformity and domesticity. Turn the channel (remember the days before TV remote controls?) and the family could watch one of the popular Westerns. In a Cold War world, Americans were reassured that the good guys would ultimately triumph over the bad guy outlaws. For the first time in history, and unlike previous generations, Boomers across America watched the same television shows and commercials. This common frame of reference helped shape our common generational view of the world.

By the 1960s, over 60 million televisions brought Americans evening news shows.[45] With the advent of news shows, Americans saw racism played out with fire hoses and police dogs, anti-war sentiment expressed with burning draft cards, and feminists burning their bras. Each evening the news brought the horror of the Vietnam War into living rooms. Americans witnessed body bags loaded onto C-141 planes and burning villages. Television "Special Reports" interrupted regularly scheduled broadcasts to bring news of three assassinations, riots burning cities, and the resignation of a US president. Amidst this national darkness, Americans did have a front row seat to the historic technological achievement of the moon landing. However, for the most part, Boomers saw a gritty reality revealing social ills across America.

Television continued to be major force in shaping Boomer social consciousness. Its importance and range grew. Compared to only 9% of American homes having television sets in 1950, by the end of the '70s 98% American homes had televisions. [46] A 1970s *TV Guide* line-up included Archie Bunker's overt bigotry, Maude's outspoken feminism, and the Jeffersons' upward mobility. Nearly all the women I interviewed cited *The Mary Tyler Moore Show* as a pivotal influence for them. After years of viewing women portrayed as maids, witches, and genies, young Boomer woman saw an attractive, unattached, single, sexually active, and successful female make inroads in the male world of broadcast news.

Boomers and television grew up together. From the idealized Golden Age of television of the 1950s to the realism of the 1960s and 1970s, the medium united and shaped our Boomer identity. It communicated the turbulence and transformations that profoundly changed the nation. It exposed Boomer women to alternative lifestyles beyond the traditional housewife or teacher or nurse roles. It emboldened Boomer women to question the status quo, ignited activism, and empowered us to reinvent our lives. As Boomer professional women, we are recycling these same behaviors to address our retirement transition.

Boomer Soundtrack: Rock and Roll

The final pivotal influence on the Boomer generation was rock and roll music. Rock and roll evolved from an eclectic combination of African-American rhythm and blues, gospel, boogie-woogie, and country music. Its beat and lyrics represented a distinct departure from the older generation's easy-listening music. Boomers had no interest in the crooner music of Frank, Bing, and Perry. Rock and roll music had a distinctive and fast beat. Its lyrics gave voice to the teenage experience, integrated racial groups, and possessed an undercurrent of sexuality and rebellion. New electric guitars magnified the sound and provided different distortion effects conveying a broad range of emotions.

The lyrics spoke directly to teenage Baby Boomers. "It echoed the vitality and feeling of separateness that animated adolescence and became the bedrock of the teenage nation. Rock was written and performed by young people and focused on what was important to them." [48] Popular songs captured the teenage dramas of school, dating, dances, and parental authority. Car radios and transistors allowed teenagers to listen to rock and roll without the critical eyes of our parents. As Boomer teenagers, we enjoyed more leisure time and discretionary money than previous generations.

Abundant new part-time jobs in new fast food restaurants and weekly allowances funded the purchase of the latest 45 records played on new portable record players. Teenagers danced to the rock and roll beat of "Be-Bop-A-Lula," "Rock Around the Clock Tonight," and "A Whole Lot of Shaking Going On."

Rock and roll music continued to evolve and reflect growing social activism in America. Railing against authority and traditional institutions, rock and roll musicians from Bob Dylan, the Beatles, the Who, and the Rolling Stones increasingly pushed beyond the mere irreverence of early rock music to advocate rebellion and revolution. Amidst this rebellious ardor, an iconic respite of peace, love, and happiness took place. A 1969 "Be-In" on a New York state farm came to symbolize the idealism and freedom espoused by many young Boomers. This watershed of Boomer rock and roll history was the Woodstock Music and Art Festival. Over 500,000 attendees "went back to the garden to set their souls free" [47] and enjoy three days of music, drugs, peace, and social activism messages. Despite shortages of food and bathroom facilities, and torrential rain, no reported incidences of violence occurred. Many Boomers view Woodstock as the highpoint of 1960s idealism. Many angry parents criticized Woodstock as a glorification of drug use, sexual immorality, and a celebration of disrespect for authority. Regardless of perspective, Woodstock helped cement rock and roll music as the soundtrack of the Boomers' coming of age. It strengthened our sense of nonconformity, desire to question authority, and activism for change.

Impacting Our World

Just as events and culture affected Boomers, given our unprecedented numbers, Boomers similarly affected the world around them. Boomers strained and changed institutions and cultural behavior from the moment they arrived on the scene.[49] Boomer impact was so pervasive that *TIME* Magazine selected this generation as its 1966 "Man of the Year." [50] Boomers were the powerful economic engine powering decades of prosperity. Enrollment in college tripled from 1965 to 1975. [51] In "numbers too big to ignore," over 70% of Boomer women worked outside the home, compared to 30% of their mothers. [52] We brought attention to environmental health issues and physical fitness. We burned draft cards and protested to successfully end a war and lower the voting age. As Boomers, we reframed the concept of work, demanding and expecting satisfaction from our jobs beyond financial security. We embraced diversity and inclusion. We questioned traditional sexual attitudes and ushered in two decades of "free love" and sexual exploration. It is against this generational backdrop, accompanied by the soundtrack of Graham Nash confirming that we can change and rearrange the world, [53] that our expectations for retirement were formed. Retirement is yet another institution Boomers will reshape and reinvent as we collectively navigate its speed bumps and explore this uncharted life stage.

The women I interviewed underscored these Boomer generational experiences as key influences in their lives and on their views of retirement. In the first interview, the impact of suburban living, television, and expanding options afforded by legal and social change are discussed. In the second interview, a woman's college experience is credited with inspiring social activism that continues to influence her today.

Boomer Women Share Their Coming-of-Age Stories

#1 Mona's* Story

Mona*, a partner in a large global consulting firm, shared her coming-of-age story with me in such vivid detail, I felt as if I had time traveled from the 1950s to the present. She elaborated on how changing media images and conjoined cultural norms shaped the direction of her life. Mona closes with reflection on how being a "first-generation female professional" and the challenges she faced as a pioneer in the male work world added complexity to her views on retirement.

"I was born in the late 1950s. My family lived in a subdivision loaded with children. I loved school. I have vague images of reading aloud from the Dick and Jane readers. In retrospect, the story lines were all about Jane watching Dick and the dog, Spot, run or play. Of course, we had our Barbie dolls. One Christmas, I received an Easy Bake Oven. We played games like Mystery Date game and Miss Popularity. My mom stayed home and took care of the house and kids, while my father went to work each day. We had one family car, a Chevy. In those days, a lot of vendors came right to the neighborhoods. There was the Joe, the Vegetable Man, the Milk Man, the Dugan Bakery Man, and the Tuscan Dairy Man.

"Powerful television images communicated what options were open to us as girls. We watched *Bewitched*, *I Dream of Jeannie*, reruns of *I Love Lucy* and *The Flying Nun*. My images of women included the magical powers of Samantha hiding her intelligence while solving problems for her clueless Darin, a sexily clad woman calling her male lead 'Master,' the comedic, clowning antics of Lucy 'splainin' herself to Ricky, and a nun who could catch a breeze and fly away. In retrospect, I think these shows hinted at the desire women had to break free of their patriarchal and oppressive situations. Of course, at the time, these women with magical powers were nothing more than an entertaining reference group for me. Working women were often portrayed as 'plain Janes,' thanklessly making male bosses look good or employed as maids. Miss Jane, from *The Beverly Hillbillies*, is the quintessential 1960s sitcom version of a career woman.

"I remember the images from the commercials, too. 'I'm Suzy, Fly Me,' the Noxema 'girl' advising to 'Take It Off, Take It All Off,' or a desperate housewife trying to remove her husband's 'Ring Around the Collar.' These messages were just accepted as the norm.

"The first signs of change for me was when *That Girl*, a single, attractive, aspiring actress, with a boyfriend, and

Mary Tyler Moore, a single, independent career woman, appeared on television. I can still recall being a seventh-grader and being truly bewildered at the life Mary Tyler Moore was living in Minneapolis. I loved, loved the show! At the time, I don't think I could articulate why I loved it so much, but now I see the freedom and possibilities the show represented. Boyfriends were secondary; relationships with women friends were no longer consolation prizes for dateless Saturday nights. Women could finally put off childbearing and work in a rewarding, professional capacity. I can honestly say because of this show, for the first time in my life, I could envision another future.

"The legal and cultural changes benefitting women seemed to snowball in the late 1960s and 1970s. In my household, my parents debated 'women's lib' at the dinner table and my older sister surreptitiously paged through *Cosmopolitan's* latest sex survey. Outside our home, Title IX education opened up school sports and other educational equities for women. In fact, I attended a university with a 200-year history of exclusively male enrollment. Women could finally have their own credit cards and apply for loans. Sexual harassment was illegal and at times went underground. There were women in Congress, women astronauts, and even a Career Barbie doll!

"Yes, there was change, but it was initially more incremental in my personal life. I majored in the traditionally feminine field of teaching. From the sidelines, I watched and cheered my boyfriend playing collegiate sports. As we came to graduation, his career as an engineer superseded any discussion of my employment or geographic preferences. Thankfully, that relationship ended right after graduation. I found teaching rewarding but couldn't stand the predominantly women faculty discussing the merits of tuna casseroles in the faculty room. I knew there had to be more than this for me.

"I went back to school and obtained an MBA, one of four women in my cohort of twenty-five students. I then left teaching, akin to leaving the priesthood for my parents, and obtained a role in business. I read *Dress for Success* and wore boxy, masculine jackets and long skirts, and neck ribbons or ties. I worked hard, eating at my desk to demonstrate my commitment. I went on business trips where the men went to watch exotic dancers and I went back to my hotel room. I was lonely. The few other women co-workers, bending to the daily pressures of a male work environment, placed competition over collegiality. The glass ceiling was real. I kept working hard and received promotions. I got married. I got divorced. I didn't have children. I traveled the world. Twenty-five years later, I finally did reach the C-Suite. I learned how to not cry at work when I was full of angry emotions. I found my voice in meetings, not allowing my male co-workers to talk over me. I won company awards.

"As I reached my fifties, though, I was tired and craved more time for my interests. Having ridden the wave of feminism in the 1970s, I was afforded more opportunity than my mom's generation. However, I felt like a battle-scarred pioneer. This made it hard for me to consider retirement.

The concept of retirement evoked feelings that I was leaving before I could declare a full victory. I had trouble envisioning retirement beyond my dad's fishing, annual trips to Florida, and reading books on the back porch. As a housewife, my poor mom never really had a formal retirement. I feared that, like my professional female friends, I would experience the regrets and the questioning that came with retirement. One of my good friends retired a year before me. As her corporate identity waned, she was surprised by feelings of regret for the many sacrifices she incurred to rise in her company. As her successors dismantled some of the programs she developed, she began to question, 'Was it worth it?' Then I began to think about what my retirement would be like. Talk about being between a rock and a hard place. I was burned out and wanted more time for me, yet I was fearful to make this happen.

"Summing up, I am grateful I was born in a time that opened up more options for women. Baby Boomer career women were truly charting new territory. My mother had limited choices. The shift from my childhood messages of limitation to the messages of possibility in my young adulthood obviously shaped my life. I am optimistic that my generation of professional women, front-line pioneers, will create possibilities for our retirement."

College Campus: Power to the People

We were the first generation not expected to go work directly after high school graduation to contribute to the family income. We could now have a four-year learning experience, away from our parents' supervision. We invaded college campuses in unprecedented numbers. Our critical mass empowered us in new ways.

In the 1950s, colleges followed the tradition of "in loco parentis" (Latin for "in place of parents") that resulted in a regulated, restricted, and segregated college system. College students were not viewed as adults. Therefore, the college was sanctioned to act as a surrogate parent.

Peering into a time capsule of 1950s college campus life, we would see young "ladies" in dresses with Peter Pan collars and young "gentlemen" wearing ties and blazers rushing to their segregated residence halls. During Freshman Orientation, the university's "Social Code Book" of acceptable social behaviors would be presented to beanie-wearing freshmen. Skimming the pages, we would see information about curfews, chaperones, dorm housemothers, restrictions on male/female inter-visitation, prohibitions of free speech, and regulations of the type of organizations on campus.

However, a few cracks in this "in loco parentis" system began to appear. In the 1950s, returning WWII GIs, leveraging the GI Bill's tuition assistance, descended on college campuses. The problem was, these students were adults. They came of age on battlefields and with the constant threat of death, experienced life at an accelerated pace. They may have left their hometowns as sheltered young men, but they came back as worldly adults. For this group, many married with children, the restrictions of "in loco parentis" were ludicrous. In addition, the growing momentum of the Civil Rights Movement furthered the questioning of restricted civil liberties for college students. With the growing disillusionment with the Vietnam War and its resultant questioning of authority, the initial fissures against the paternal, restrictive college system, widened into a fault line of resistance against "in loco parentis." Eventually legal challenges to infringement of civil liberties brought "in loco parentis" to an end.

When overcrowded college campuses, relaxed supervision, and socially aware students came together, a powerful nexus of protest and activism was unleashed.

Boomer Women Share Their Coming-of-Age Stories

#2 Kathy's* Story

When I spoke with Kathy*, an SVP Engineering for a manufacturing company, she reflected on how her college activism was influential in her lifelong distrust for the "Establishment" and her questioning and drive for change. She laughed at how forty years later, she was approaching her retirement with this same questioning attitude and a desire to change the status quo.

"I entered college in 1972, in the first co-ed class at my Ivy League school. Dorms were still segregated by gender, but gone were the curfews, housemothers, and restrictions on coed visitation. There were no sororities, and women's sports was in its infancy. There was no such thing as

Women's Studies programs. The smell of pot regularly wafted down the dorm halls. Rock music was a constant. To this day, when I hear Deep Purple's 'Smoke on the Water' playing, I am transported back to my freshman dorm. This was a far cry from my mother's college experience in the early 1950s. In retrospect, I can't imagine what my parents were thinking as they left me with my boxes and orange Pinto.

"Given the social freedom and the intellectual stimulation college afforded me, I did become active in various "anti-Establishment" causes. This was a crazy time with the Vietnam War. The number of US troops was declining, but this was misleading. One minute, Nixon had Kissinger in peace talks with North Vietnam, and the next minute he was ordering his generals to conduct massive carpet-bombing. This only deepened our distrust for the government. Of course, remaining trust and faith in the Establishment later took a nosedive with Watergate.

"I participated in a few anti-war marches, including taking a bus to a huge march in Washington. I truly believed the Vietnam War was illegal and our government was lying to us. I made posters, collected signatures for petitions, and wore my peace sign button. I was not, however, chaining myself to the administration building and or throwing rocks at National Guard troops. Actually, these types of activists really were a minority.

"When the book *Our Bodies, Ourselves* hit the stores, it was avidly passed around the dorm. In essence, it was advocating women to claim their sexuality for their own pleasure. And it had diagrams and pictures! Now a feminist classic, the book discussed formally taboo subjects like mas-turbation, abortion, and lesbianism. All the 'nice girls save themselves' propaganda flew out the dorm window. By my junior year, I was in a steady relationship and on the Pill. Roe v. Wade further created the reality of 'choice' for women.

"My two heroines at the time were political activ-ists 'Battling' Bella Abzug, US Representative, and Gloria Steinem. I savored every article in Gloria's newly launched *Ms. Magazine*. I was derisively called a 'Women's Libber' and a 'Feminist' by the frat guys. My mom advised me to be less outspoken about women's liberation, as it would scare off potential husband material. I think that ship had already sailed when I became one of the few females in the Engineering School! The problem was that I was angry and passionate to my core about women's rights. I collected a petition of 2,500 names in support of the Equal Rights Amendment and sent it to our Congressman. I participated in rallies. I was a founding member of a women's political caucus on campus. Of course, I knew every word to Helen Reddy's 'I Am Woman, Hear Me Roar.' Even after graduating college, I've always been outspoken on women's rights. My experiences climbing the career ladder in patriarchal corpo-rations served to keep my women's rights activism alive. It is well known that women earn less than men for comparable work. With retirement on my mind, I've been reading more and more on the cumulative effective of this wage gap im-pacting women in retirement. Earning less than men over their working careers forces women to stretch their retire-ment funds further than men.

"Which brings me to my aging and upcoming retirement. First of all, I love that Boomers just won't accept aging and intervene in every way possible. Botox, fillers, personal trainers, hair dye, are all part of my fountain of youth routine. Secondly, it doesn't surprise me that my generation is questioning the old 'sit-in-the-rocking chair' models of retirement. We were weaned on self-fulfillment and questioning the status quo. We entered adulthood in a turbulent time and we drove change as activists. Now I kind of see myself as a retirement activist, reinventing my retirement experience."

Change: A Part of Boomer DNA

Both Mona and Kathy's recounting the experiences that shaped them are representative of the hundreds of women I interviewed. Baby Boomers grew up in two very different eras. Our childhoods of tradition and conformity matured into a period characterized by defiance and reform. Our upbringing influenced our sense of entitlement, self-fulfillment, and questioning of authority. As teenagers and young adults, we played this out with activism, protests, and optimism that we could change the world. In the decades that followed, Boomers moved into adulthood, careers, family, and much of this bias toward questioning the Establishment and reinventing institutions went dormant. However, it was imprinted in our generational DNA. As Boomer professional women, when we embark on our retirement, these strands of defiance and change are reactivated.

TAKING TIME TO REFLECT:

4. How has my coming of age in the 1960s and 1970s influence how I view my retirement?

5. To what extent am I connected to my generation's professional career women for support?

6. Going back to the 1960s and 1970s, what ideals, dreams, or beliefs have gone dormant in me over the years?

CHAPTER 3

"SOUND OF SILENCE"

(Simon and Garfunkel)

Midlife's Vortex of Empty Nests, Aging, and Retirement

The Middle Ages

For a generation obsessed with youth, Boomers are particularly challenged by the complexities of midlife. After all, this is the generation who youthfully advised "never trust anyone over thirty." Boomer era rock and roll anthems describe dread and even confusion about growing old. Pete Townsend's lyrics "Hope I die before I get old" (The Who, 1965) captures the Boomers' incomprehension of growing old. Would Boomers end up like the tragic, aging rock and roll star in Jethro Tull's (1976) "Too old to rock n' roll, too young to die"? Midlife, approximately between forty and sixty-five years of age, brings forth both biological and psychological changes to the aging Boomer. Children leave home, leaving an "empty nest" behind them. Most midlife adult children experience the profound impact of the death of a parent or parents. Physical limitations and age-related illnesses appear. For women, menopause is the biological marker for the loss of fertility in a childbearing-focused society. All these midlife transitions occur simultaneous with Boomer professional women contemplating or embarking on one of life's biggest transitions--retirement.

The concept of "middle age" is a relatively new phenomenon. In the 1950s, psychologist Erik Erickson popularized the idea that life is defined by stages versus key events like marriage and parenthood. In 1974, author Gail Sheehy leveraged Erikson's work in her bestselling book *Passages: Predictable Crises of Adult Life.* Sheehy associated each passage with common changes and challenges for adults resulting in self-examination and transformation. [54]. Responses to "middle age" range from grief of perceived losses to celebrating this period as an opportunity. Regardless of the response, this period is a clearly a transition. Boomer women are part of the first generation to enter into our forties and fifties after the Second-Wave Feminism, and we have options our mothers and grandmothers could barely imagine. [55] While choices represent freedom and opportunity, the range of choices also contributes to the complexity of mid-life issues.

Goodbye, Mommy

Every year, millions of Boomer women drop off their youngest child at college or see them off to military boot camp. We go home to a silent house, an empty chair at the dinner table, and a blank activity schedule on the refrigerator. Clearly this signals the end of our job of active, day-to-day mothering. While reactions to this experience are highly individualized, there are enough commonalities to refer to this phase of life as the "empty nest syndrome." Common responses include a sense of bereavement, loss of identity, disorientation, and a feeling of redundancy. Some Boomer women report a duality of emotions, going back and forth from grief to excitement. In *The Happy Empty Nest: Rediscovering Love and Success After Your Kids Leave Home*, author Linda Burghardt estimated that approximately 75% of the parents she spoke to suffered from some symptoms of the empty nest syndrome.[56] Again, the depth and tenure of these responses vary among women.

The term "syndrome" is actually misnomer. Pick up a copy of the DSM (*Diagnostic and Statistical Manual of Mental Disorders*) published by the American Psychiatric Association (APA), and note that the "empty nest syndrome" is not classified as a clinical diagnosis in this tome. The empty nest syndrome more accurately describes a transition phase. Historically, women's midlife transitions have been described in derogatory and patronizing terms. The empty nest syndrome is no exception. The image of the empty nest evokes images of poor, sad birds. Society has been preoccupied with using the "language of the barnyard" when referring to women (e.g. "birds, chicks, old hens") perpetuating sexist and ageist attitudes.[57] A more neutral terminology, which I will use in the remainder of this chapter, is the term "post-parental period."[58]

When did the concept of the post-parental period become part of the collective consciousness? How does it contribute to Boomer professional women's midlife experience? What effect could the post-parental period have on the planning and launching of retirement for these women?

The concept of a post-parental period in the United States emerged in the later part of the 20th century. In the 1900s, before the advent of and access to reliable birth control, women bore children into their mid-forties. The lifespan for these women averaged fifty or sixty years. Children typically lived at home until marriage. After the last child left home, the 1900s woman experienced a relatively small number of post-parental years. However, as life expectancy increased over the course of the 20th century, the average lifespan for women reached eighty-four years of age, yielding a much longer post-parental period. Beginning in the 1960s, "the Pill" allowed women to delay childbirth. For many Boomer women, this delay resulted in the intersection of their reaching middle age at the same time their children were leaving home for college, the military, or careers. The post-parental period lasts decades longer for Boomer women than it did for their grandmothers. Carin Rubenstein, author of *Beyond the Mommy Years: How to Live Happily Ever After...After the Kids Leave Home*, aptly describes this elongated period for Boomers as not just a brief chapter of adult life, but rather a whole new book.[59]

For Boomer women, one of the largest impacts of middle age is a loss of our motherhood role and the identity associated with this role. The day-to-day motherhood role that occupied over twenty years is, in essence, retired. Children leaving home for their adult lives certainly affects their fathers; however, their mothers tend to be more impacted. Women tend to bear more child-rearing responsibilities. This impact is compounded if the woman is a single mother. In my interviews, women also shared missing the collegiality with other mothers and the engagement with previous child-centered activities. Gone were the Friday Night Lights high school football games and band fundraisers. Gone was chauffeuring a gaggle of teenagers around town. Gone was a leadership role with the PTO, Parent-Teacher's Organization.

Launching our children into adulthood, many Boomer women are simultaneously launching themselves into retirement. The post-parental period and retirement displace the familiar roles and identities of motherhood and work professional. Women find themselves adjusting to the loss of two foundational roles at the same time. Ironically, studies show that women who are active workforce professionals suffer less distress during the post-parental period than women who are not employed or employed in less career-oriented roles. [60] Career women are more heavily invested in an alternative role beyond the motherhood role. Boomer professional women must be aware of and carefully tread this tight wire of opposing forces.

Adult Orphans

As Boomers travel through midlife, nearly all of us will experience the loss of our parents. The death of a parent changes people profoundly at any age, and it is surprisingly disorienting for middle-aged adult children. Just as other transitions engulf middle-aged Boomer women, the death of our parents is added to the mix. Adult orphanhood brings new responsibilities, an altered worldview, and a new role.

One of the key insights for middle-aged Boomers is the realization that half or more of life is behind them. We are beginning to sense our own mortality. However, when parents die, the surviving adult child crosses the generational line, assuming the position of next to die. Emotional denial and clinging to immortality falls to the wayside. Gone is the parental insulation that psychologically buffered the adult child from the possibility of their own death. [61] With the passing of their parents, Boomer women lose our role as child and instantly become a family elder. We are now responsible for family traditions, transferring family history, and being a source of wisdom for our extended families. Many of the women I interviewed reported that their role shift, with its increased adult responsibilities, felt akin to getting a promotion--albeit a promotion which they did not want and for which they felt unprepared.

As Boomer professional women begin earnestly contemplating the major life transition of retirement, we feel the void left by our parents' passing. With other major life transitions, our parents were always available to provide insight and emotional support. With our parents' passing, adult orphans lose their "wisdom keepers" [62] and the prime archivists of their lives. [63] After spending a lifetime looking to our parents for answers on everything from child-rearing to family history, Boomers are forced into the stark reality of a new level of self-sufficient adulthood.

Some adult children are faced with unresolved parental issues. Feelings of finality, frustration, anger, and remorse accompany their grief. Some who served as caretakers for our parents feel guilt over their relief and sense of freedom. A handful of women I interviewed described feeling uncomfortable over their inheritance. Overnight we can inherit what took their parents a lifetime to accumulate.[64] Spending this money can be bittersweet.

The loss of parents is natural part of the human life cycle. However, the timing for Boomer professional women typically coincides with losing our motherhood role and additional aging challenges. Add to this the transition of retirement.

As Time Goes By

For some of us, there is a defining moment when aging becomes a reality. For others it is a cluster of events. Amidst the birthday cards Boomers receive on their 50th birthday, they see *IT*. Our AARP membership card (American Association of Retired People) sits on top of our pile of mail, undeniably welcoming us to senior citizen status. Or perhaps their "wake-up call" was when the doctor advised them to start getting colonoscopies at age fifty. Maybe it was hearing our favorite rock and roll classics turned into bland elevator music. Boomers are struggling with the concept of their aging. In fact, Boomers are always up for creative reinvention of institutions, have redefined old age. Sixty is becoming the new fifty and forty the new thirty, and so on. Our mothers and grandmothers, however, viewed aging as a natural and normal process--not as something they could control, delay or even stop.[65] Throughout my interviews, I heard the lament: "But I feel too young to be old."

Growing up in the 1950s, 1960s, and early 1970s, Boomers experienced many life improvement and life extension innovations in medicine. To name a few: the pacemaker (1958) ,dialysis (1960), CPR (1960), hip replacement (1962), soft contact lenses (1965), heart transplant (1967), the artificial heart (1969), the CT scanner (1973), and the MRI (1973). It appeared there was no limit to the innovation and inventions that could launch an assault on the aging process. Boomers, therefore, have innate optimism toward medical science to provide anti-aging solutions. In 2017, the US spends on cosmetic treatments and surgery is approximately $15 billion dollars per year.[66]

Boomers are simply not willing to accept the inevitability of traditional old age. Today, Boomers can avail themselves to an arsenal of anti-aging weapons such as Botox, liposuction, chemical peels, cool sculpting, chemical fillers,

face lifts, tummy tucks, anti-cellulite treatment, hair resto-
ration, teeth implants, and laser eye surgery. Don't forget
banishing gray hair. In 1956, Clairol boldly advertised their
hair-coloring dye with the campaign: "Does She or Doesn't
She? Only Her Hairdresser Knows for Sure." Previously, hair
coloring was for chorus girls and starlets, but not "nice
women." If "nice women" could overcome their fears about
hair dye chemicals, they would sneak through hair salons'
discreet back doors to color their hair. In the early 1950s,
only 7% of women older than forty colored their hair; today
that statistic may be as high as 75%.[67] Ironically, many of the
same people who, in the 1960s, were "setting their souls
free" and "getting back to the garden" [68] are now injecting a
highly toxic poison (botulinum toxin-Botox) into their fore-
heads. Perhaps this is a testament to the battles youth-obsessed Boomers are willing to wage against aging.

In the early 1970s, at a feminist workshop entitled
"Women and Their Bodies," women discussed their personal health and sexuality. They shared this information with
doctors in attendance. Their mission was to share information about women's unique health issues and to challenge
the medical establishment to change and improve healthcare for women. The knowledge was collected into the
widely popular, award-winning book, *Our Bodies, Ourselves:
A Book By and For Women*. This book was revolutionary for
the times. It frankly and graphically talked about topics like
abortion (illegal at the time), birth control, childbirth, domestic violence, sexual orientation, and menopause. This
book encouraged women to own their reproductive health

and to view their sexuality as a source of their own pleasure. This book, with ongoing revisions, is still in print.

For the first time, discussions of menopause moved from muffled whispers and arcane references to the "change of life." As Boomer women age, we are more informed and willing to discuss the biological and psychological changes menopause brings. Women are typically relieved to be free of their menstrual cycles, the accompanying symptoms and inconveniences. At the same time, menopause is a definitive milestone of aging. Many women view the end of fertility as yet another loss in their middle-age years. Recent studies have found strong evidence that menopause may actually accelerate aging in women.[69] Disclaimer: the following menopause symptoms of aging may be considered rather depressing to middle-aged Boomer women. Reader discretion is advised! Beyond the ubiquitous hot flashes, skin becomes dry, more wrinkles appear, gray hair increases, weakening eyesight, weight gain is common, muscle loss occurs, facial hair appears, vaginal atrophy makes sexual intercourse painful, sleep is interrupted, bones become more fragile, there is higher risk of heart disease, and some memory loss appears. Boomer women realize their bodies are betraying them in a youth-obsessed culture. Just like in their youth, a candid resource exists to support them through this change. Boomer women can now add *Our Bodies, Ourselves: Menopause* to their library. This book provides frank and detailed information to help women navigate menopause. Published in 2006, forty years after the Baby

Boom began, it is targeted at Boomer women who previously viewed *Our Bodies, Ourselves* as their feminist bible. Congruent with our generational DNA, Boomer women are questioning the status quo of female aging and raising their voices for change. There is no doubt that we will continue to reshape menopause.

Despite this empowered approach to menopause, Boomer professional women, having lived through decades of sexism, are now stepping into a new "ism": ageism. Many of the women I interviewed describe this ageism as a feeling of being "invisible." This manifests in both the workplace and in their personal lives. At work, they are passed over for promotions, viewed as less innovative, and find it difficult to get new jobs for which they are highly qualified. On a personal level, they perceive they are no longer viewed as young and desirable. They grew up in a society that put premiums on their youth and sexual appeal. Facing yet another loss, women often struggle to redefine and regain their sense of self. Self-confidence is shaken.

The Vortex: Empty Nest, Aging, and Retirement

The confluence of women losing our parental role, our parental support system, moving out of denial regarding tour own mortality, and experiencing physical signs of aging are happening just as we are planning the last portion of our adult lives. On one hand, confidence is shaken, and we experience the grief of losing people and roles. On the other hand, the physical signs of aging and loss of our parents are catalysts forcing us to come face to face with mortality. This can shake a complacent Boomer into a sense of urgency and importance to create a retirement lifestyle that provides meaning and purpose to her life. This is our last chance to "get it right."

The stories that follow illustrate how Boomer professional women deal with various aspects of middle age and its effect on their retirement planning and retirement itself.

Boomer Women Share Their Midlife Challenges

#1 Allison

Many women, like Allison*, a corporate attorney, reported experiencing a range of emotions, from excitement and pride for her daughter, sadness to see her leave home, and surprising moments of grief regarding her own downshifting stage of life.

"It was during our traditional college freshman pilgrimage to the local big box bedding and bath store that the reality of Leslie's leaving hit me. My daughter excitedly held up her 'bed-in-a-bag' selection and talked about her roommate and dorm room décor. I plastered a smile on my face to hide my growing sadness that my youngest child was truly leaving home and was stepping into adulthood. I would miss the energy she brought to our home. I would miss being able to guide and comfort her on a daily basis. I would miss the boyfriend dramas. I would miss her 'girl gang' laughing around our kitchen table. I'm sure my smile shifted to a frown when I wondered how our relationship would change. In the last few years, a friendship beyond the bounds of parenthood was emerging between Leslie and myself. My inner dialogue was interrupted by Leslie asking for my opinion on a desk lamp."

Allison continued to describe her mixed emotions. "I am proud of the person Leslie has become. She has her head on straight. She is bright and confident. Her whole wonderful future lies ahead. At age sixty-one, my future is in a reverse trajectory. I retire next year. My primary identities as a mom and an attorney are coming to a close. I have trouble reconciling all my emotions: sadness over Leslie's leaving home, pride for her accomplishments and promise of a bright future, and grief for my own life downshifts. Then mix in a few hot flashes and hormonal moodiness. I know my husband is confused by my mixed bag of emotions. Hell, I'm confused by my mixed bag of emotions!"

Boomer Women Share Their Midlife Challenges

#2 Lenora

I also discovered women uncomfortably vacillating between polarized emotions, voicing guilt for wanting more time for themselves. Lenora*, a community college administrator and just months from retiring, shared, "Of course I'm sad to see my youngest child leave home. There is ten years between my oldest and youngest. I've already launched three of my children into the world. I've experienced the immediate void, worries about their adjustments to college or a new career, and renegotiating my role in their new life. Of course I will miss my son. But I need to be really honest here; my husband and I are also happily looking forward to our freedom from day-to-day parenthood. I am almost embarrassed to say this out loud. Don't get me wrong; we were good, involved parents and our children all graduated college and have good careers. I worked throughout our child-rearing years, with the exception of a five-year sabbatical when my children were young. My life was basically work and our kids, both of which I loved. Time management became an art form for me. However, as I entered my fifties, I had a growing feeling of wanting more time to feed my personal passions. I would love to get back to my art, travel without my briefcase full of work, volunteer, or maybe take courses. Before our children arrived, Dave and I had a wonderfully exciting marriage, traveling to exotic locales. I look forward to rekindling this closeness and sense of adventure. Is it selfish of me to feel excited about my empty nest? Usually I don't share much about this with people for fear they will judge me as a really cold person. A good friend of mine has a daughter who has moved back home after a divorce. What do they call this trend? Yeah, I think they call this the 'boomerang generation.' Who knows; my empty nest may turn into a full house again. Wouldn't that be ironic?"

Boomer Women Share Their Midlife Challenges

#3 Kathy

I also spoke with Boomer professional women who experienced guilt and regret for career sacrifices that impacted their children. Retirement itself creates a reflective distance from our careers. Often, we are irrationally surprised by how easily we are replaced and how our department thrives without us. Simultaneously we are at a life stage, triggered by retirement, when we examine our life's meaning and purpose. Retirement, coupled with an "empty nest," can result in a vortex of regret and guilt over every dinner, school event and winning game missed. Kathy*, a Human Resources executive and single parent, shared her complex struggle with guilt and regret.

"I was caught off-guard by the depth and persistence of the guilt I felt after my daughter graduated and moved to New York City. I had always believed that my career success provided a strong role model for my daughter. I felt I had balanced my own fulfillment for a career with being a good mother. Of course, there were times I had guilt when work prevented me from being there for her. I remember flying all night to Brussels and picking up my voicemail messages in the taxi en route to the hotel. My mother called to tell me my infant daughter was running a fever. An ocean separated me from my sick baby. My mother took her to the doctor, and the baby rallied quickly. But to this day, as I relate this story, I can feel that awful feeling of anxiety in the pit of my stomach and questioning my abilities as a mother. But over-all, I felt that the positives of my career success, my being a role model, and the lifestyle it afforded us were acceptable trade-offs.

"I definitely struggled with being marginalized by my former work colleagues and the whole identity issues that came with my retirement. Then once I had the proverbial empty nest, I began to replay my child-rearing and career years through the filter of time lost forever. Was speaking at that international conference really worth missing my daughter's first varsity soccer game? I tortured myself with regret and insecurity about my choices. On some level, I realized that the magnitude of my feelings was extreme. I spoke with my daughter, who reassured me that I was there when it counted. But I just couldn't move her reassurances from my head to my heart. Intellectually, I know that regret and guilt are toxic emotions. I'm currently seeing a therapist to help me move through this."

Boomer Women Share Their Midlife Challenges

#4 Brooke

Finally, I include thoughts expressed by Brooke*, a six-ty-four-year-old financial services executive, regarding the tremendous feelings of loss arising in her midlife years. Her grieving was real. She recognized that she needed to work through this before she could embark on a self-fulfilling and meaningful retirement.

"I honestly hate getting old! After all the years I complained about wolf whistles from construction workers, I have to confess, just one more wolf whistle would be nice today. I live on lettuce, shoot up my face with Botox, and obsessively exercise. It is a losing battle. My husband is a sweetheart and says he doesn't notice me getting older. I know he is just being kind. I must spend thousands a year on anti-aging creams. At work, I am told I have 'limited runway,' a talent management term for no more promotions in my future. I'm on the high end of the pay scale, which translates into wearing a target on my back should my company have layoffs. My younger co-workers assume I am a technical dinosaur. I am invisible to most of the world. Once in a while, I am appreciated as the voice of seasoned wisdom.

"Over the past five years, I've lost both my parents. This was such a profound, life-changing experience for me. I miss them every single day. My life cheerleaders are gone. I am instantly the elder in my family. My family looks to me to provide the glue to keep us all together. This is a responsibility I really don't want. My husband and I don't have children, so at least we aren't experiencing cutting the cord with children leaving home. However, as I see the realities of my getting old, I do wonder who will take care of me.

"Depressing—right? It's just that it feels like it all came at once. Sometimes I feel death is right around the corner for me. With the relatively short time left, what do I want to do, become? I'm sorting through it all, seeing a grief counselor and working to acknowledge my grief. I want to retire next year, but just haven't been in the right mind frame to really plan the non-financial stuff. I am gaining more acceptances of the losses and trying to reframe this normal life stage progression as part of the human existence. I'm trying to use the losses to kick my butt into creating an amazing last act for myself."

For most of the women I interviewed, the complexity of the "vortex" was a surprise. Our midlife changes and challenges occur against the backdrop of entering the uncharted territory of retirement as Baby Boomer career women. We are moving from balancing multiple roles to adjusting to a sense of being marginalized. Former "have-it-all Wonder Women" are letting go of our enchanted golden lassos, bullet-proof bracelets and red winged boots. Within this new void, the question "What next?" begins as a quiet whisper and increasingly grows into an unrelenting shout.

TAKING TIME TO REFLECT:

1. How do I feel about being at this stage in my life?

2. What are the positives? What are the negatives?

3. What can I do more of, less of, or stop in relation to managing my mid-life?

CHAPTER 4

"EIGHT DAYS A WEEK"

(The Beatles)

Saying Goodbye to Power and Perks

For a majority of professionals, job title and identity are indistinguishable from one another. Over the years, immersed in a work system that rewards a "take no prisoners" work ethic, we slowly lose their authentic selves. If this loss of self seems a dramatic overstatement, just ask a newly retired professional the seemingly innocuous cocktail party question, "So what do you do?" Note the uncomfortable look on the retiree's face, their stammering, and their mumbling something about "I used to..." telegraphing the void created by retirement. Professional identities provide a surprising amount of structure, purpose, status, power, rewards, recognition, productivity, social community, and a host of "perks." Over the years, powerful perks blind us to our loss of identity. Only from the perspective of retirement can we see how much of our identity is defined by our careers. Looking in the rearview mirror of our careers, we can now clearly see what we lost when we stepped into retirement. Preoccupied with this view of loss, it is difficult for us to look forward through the windshield to what is next for us.

It is challenging for any professional to relinquish their career lifestyle; however, for Boomer professional women it is uniquely more complex and challenging. Historically, we are the first women to reach professional and leadership roles. We are the first generation of women to work long enough to experience the former male world of retirement. As Boomer professional women, we have a unique work history; we have faced institutional barriers and lived with daily inequities. Despite our disproportionate home responsibilities, we advanced up the career ladder. Over the course of our career ride, we grasped the brass ring of success. For decades we adapted to more highly valued "male" leadership traits, competed on uneven ground, and constantly worked to "prove ourselves." After inching our way up the career ladder, it is very difficult to walk away from the hard-earned brass ring.

Climbing the Career Ladder in Heels

Professional career roles are so much more than just work. They convey an all-encompassing lifestyle. As Boomer women entered the ranks of doctors, dentists, lawyers, accountants, and executives, we experienced the status, power, and money found at this rarefied level of success. With six- and seven- figure earning power, we entered the ranks of the top 1% of earners in the United States. Despite the inequities of male versus female wages, our earnings still became a tangible scorecard of our success. We drove luxury cars, wore designer clothes, and took amazing vacations. We purchased increasingly larger homes. Retail therapy became an outlet for the stress of our careers. The salespeople at St. Johns Knits or Louis Vuitton knew us by name. We employed people to clean our homes. We threw items into our shopping carts with barely a glance at the price tag. Our children attended private school.

At work, we moved into larger offices. We were awarded prime parking real estate. Our executive assistants kept us organized and productive. They reminded us to go to the dentist, get a yearly exam, and send flowers to a sick friend. We traveled the world to conduct business. We used our elite frequent flyer status to board airplanes before the masses. We comfortably settled into business-class or first-class seats. We slept in luxury hotels on 1,000-thread Egyptian cotton sheets. The press of the room service speed dial button quickly addressed our hunger.

We were in control, making rapid-fire leadership decisions. Our organizational charts were concrete maps of our power. We were surrounded with people who sought to leverage our power. There were the constant stimuli of problem- solving, surmounting the next work challenge, and being part of the inner power circle. Clutching our Blackberries, we felt vital. We received recognition and rewards for our efforts.

Boomer Work Ethic

The power and perks of professional careers feed the Boomer generation's achievement orientation, competitiveness, consumerism, and need for instant gratification. After all, we grew up in an age of affluence, competing against historic numbers of peers, child-focused parenting, and seemingly endless possibilities. Unlike our parents' generation, hard work is a badge of honor and not driven primarily by necessity. Internet searches on the term "Baby Boomers" frequently use the descriptor "workaholics" to describe our generation.

"Workaholic," defined as valuing work over any other activity, is a term frequently used to describe Baby Boomers.

The American cultural value of hard work was coded into our nation's DNA centuries before the arrival of the Boomer generation. As the Puritans stepped on to the shores of what is now Massachusetts, they brought with them a belief that self-reliance, hard work, material wealth, and thrift were signs of God's blessing. Other nations are confounded by the premium Americans place on long work hours. According to a 2016 International Labor Office report, "Americans work 260 hours per year more than British workers and over 499 hours more per year than French workers. We even work 137 more than the Japanese, known for their extreme work ethic. [70] Surpassing the notoriously long work hours in Japan is a dubious accomplishment. The Japanese are the only culture whom has an actual word (karoshi) that means "death by overwork." However, as Boomers, we elevated the American cultural heritage of hard work and achievement to new levels of addiction.

It may appear ironic that many Boomers, who rejected their fathers 1950s-1960s "Organization Man" identity, went onto value 60-hour workweeks and to embrace consumerism. First of all, most Boomers' rejection of their fathers' lifestyles was more a rejection of the mind-numbing conformity of their work organizations and suburban values. Boomers rejected institutional hypocrisy, constricting moral values, and the destructive impact progress had on the environment. Plus it was a "cool" youth rite of passage to adopt counterculture attitudes and dress. In actuality, very few Boomers fully relinquished the comforts of suburban life and settled permanently in communes. As Boomers entered the maturity of adulthood, we modified our belief system to include working for "the man," albeit while seeking meaningful work, and to extend our competitive streak to consumerism.

Hippie to Yuppie

Founded by a Baby Boomer, Starbucks is a quintessential example of this dichotomy of work and profits with a humanistic, counter-culture value system. Born in 1953, its founder, Howard Schultz, unabashedly built a global company worth more than $15 billion in annual revenue while incorporating Boomer values. Shades of Boomer thinking are evident in Starbucks' company values of *"challenging the status quo"* and *"performance driven, through the lens of humanity."*[71]

Like Schultz, a majority of our Boomer generation migrated from tie-dye t-shirts and doing our own thing to wearing business suits and acquiring our own things. Competing and acquiring easily slip into "workaholism." We did so while still trying to preserve our values of embracing change, searching for meaning, and keeping our planet green.

Boomer Work Ethic

Boomer "workaholism" came at a price, though. We grew up "having everything" and we expected to "have everything" in our adult lives. We wanted successful and meaningful careers, to raise high-achieving children, and have all the toys and amenities our success could buy. Somewhere along the way, this "have everything" quest imploded. We found ourselves in a circular quest for work/life balance and for many, experiencing the highest divorce rate in history. Further disillusionment came with economic slowdown, subsequent job losses, and the flattening of organizational career ladders. Today, Generation Xers and Millennials, having witnessed the impact of "workaholism" and the tenuous nature of economic security, openly reject the Boomers' "have everything" mindset and lifestyle.

Perseverance and Cracks in the Glass Ceiling

When most Boomer women professionals entered the professional work world, the newspaper want ads had separate listings for men and women. Female- intensive work choices available to the majority of women included being a nurse, teacher, librarian, or social worker. Getting pregnant could get you fired. Civil Rights legislation marked the beginning of legal changes. Title IX legislation threw out gender quotas and opened the doors for more women to access both college and advanced degrees. Additional government mandates continued to drive change. In 1973, the Supreme Court ruled that sex-segregated employment was illegal. In 1979, the Pregnancy Discrimination Act was passed. Social changes on the heels of the anti-Vietnam War movement and widespread use of the Pill similarly altered women's career expectations. Rather than attend college to pursue traditional female careers or the derogatory "Mrs." Degree, women began to select college majors reflecting their expanded expectations. Women sought careers as lawyers, accountants, doctors, college professors, engineers, and business managers.

Armed with our professional degrees, Boomer women entered a workforce where masculine norms ruled. We slogged through the unfamiliar territory of autocratic hierarchies where competitiveness valued over cooperation, and assertive communication was expected. The male leadership traits were not part of our DNA wiring or socialization experiences. Our strengths of collaboration, inclusivity, persuasion, and multi-tasking were dismissed. We attempted to understand the communication shorthand of sports analogies. We felt the social isolation as we watched our male colleagues bond over rounds of golf. We awkwardly declined to join the all-male group at an adult entertainment bar after our group dinner. We persevered.

We caught the disapproving side glances when we left work to be home in time for family dinner and supervision of homework. We donned our superwoman capes. The popular fragrance commercial of the 1970's became our default anthem, declaring "we bring home the bacon, fry it up in a pan, and never, ever, ever let you forget you're a man." We looked for answers in the new *Working Woman* and *Working Mother* magazines. We persevered.

We tried hard to adapt to this strange and exclusive world. We had no role models. Our mothers were typically homemakers. We tried to become "one of the guys." The shoulder pads on our suits shouted masculinity and morphed our physiques into that of football linebackers. We wore ribbon neckties and long, boxy skirts, simultaneously adopting male characteristics and sublimating our femininity. Rather than use lunch as an opportunity for networking, we worked through lunches in an effort to prove ourselves. We pretended we did not hear sexually harassing remarks. Often we were the only women in meetings. Or as the only woman in a meeting, we were initially viewed as an assistant and even asked to serve coffee or make copies. We persevered.

We witnessed less-qualified male counterparts receive promotions. Our career paths were handicapped by a double-bind standard of leadership qualities. We were told to be more aggressive and less sensitive. When we were more aggressive and less sensitive, we were viewed as "bitches." In the work environment of high competitiveness and devaluation of female characteristics, we viewed other female professionals warily. We became increasingly aware that we were paid less for the same work performed by our male counterparts. If we took maternity leave, we were sidelined as being on the "Mommy Track." We persevered.

Our perseverance paid off. We eventually did climb the rungs up steep career ladders. We were chagrined when younger generations of women dismissed or failed to acknowledge the pioneering path we paved for them. The reality is that they offer little appreciation of our jumping hurdles and breaking through barriers thwarting our groundbreaking entry into the male bastions of professional careers. We felt anger stirring--anger at how we had to adapt to a male work world. We invested and sacrificed so much to achieve our success. As we prepare for or enter into retirement, we feel a unique loss beyond what our male counterparts experience. Yes, we lose our corporate identity when we retire. But we also grieve the enormous emotional and financial costs of the inequities we faced decade after decade. As Boomer professional women, we add this grief to the other identity losses professionals and executives (men and women) experience when they step into retirement.

Who Am I Now?

Regardless of how much we liked or disliked our career role, we are still blindsided by the impact of leaving a professional work world that defined us for most of our adult lives. Our purpose and importance, in large part defined by our careers, enters an unfamiliar abyss. Over the decades of our careers, we ultimately failed to comprehend that our professional career roles are temporary identities.

Our perceived indispensable importance is crashed against the rocks when we visit our former workplace. The new security guard does not recognize us. Our former purposeful strides through familiar hallways of power are gone. As former employees, we must be escorted through these hallways and/or wear the anonymous badge of "Visitor." Miraculously, the company has thrived without us. We feel the sting of being marginalized upon hearing that our successor dismantled a few of our signature initiatives. Former co-workers stop for a moment to say hello, but dash off to their important meetings. Even in the few short months since we left the organization, more and more faces are unfamiliar. We may experience polite introductions to these new employees. However, we are ultimately as irrelevant to them as the fading portrait gallery of old, male executives adorning the board room walls.

As the constant text and email alerts turn silent, we know we are truly settling into retirement. Although initially relieved, if not elated, by finally having undisturbed time, this silence can become deafening. Our electronic calendars reveal a majority of white space, peppered with a few medical and personal upkeep appointments. We discover that much of our social network was our "work family." In most cases, after our bonds to the mutual organization are cut, we find little in common. Holiday cards from our "work family" slow to a trickle. In some cases, we are fortunate to have cultivated enduring collegial friendships. We learned, though, that these are far rarer than we previously expected.

We sit on a precarious fault line of change. All aspects of our life are shifting: friends, status, renegotiating family roles in retirement, rewards, career perks, and our overall sense of purpose and importance. Without our professional careers, who are we? Who will we become?

What's Next?

This profound question of identity comes at a time of life when we are aging, and our own mortality begins peaking over the horizon of our retirement. Our single-minded career focus provided little time and space, beyond a glance at a financial statement, to design our retirement lifestyles. "There is this idea that we will wake up at sixty-seven and now we can put on a different set of clothes and do something different. But then you suddenly realize, 'I never thought through who I was because I was so busy earning a living.'"[72]

The two accounts that follow encapsulate the identity shock retirement can bring Boomer professional women. In the first account, Liz* shares making peace with her resentment at the unequal sacrifices she made throughout her careers. In the second account, Debbie* courageously shares the adjustment challenges and depression she experienced upon her retirement. Like so many Boomer professional women, Liz* and Debbie* never imagined their long-awaited retirement would be fraught with psychological challenges.

Boomer Women Share Their Retirement Shock Stories

#1 Liz

Liz* was newly retired when interviewed. She served as Group Executive Vice President of a global, European-based financial services company in her last role prior to retirement. Liz* has one son and has been happily married for thirty years.

"I retired six months ago. My husband is still working. My son is newly married and lives a couple hours away. Probably like everyone else with whom you've spoken, I looked forward to retirement. Working for a company headquartered in Europe dictated an enormous amount of travel for me. For a middle-class kid from Long Island, I did get to see the world. My career provided me with financial wealth and experiences I could never have dreamed of as I rollerskated down the streets of Levittown. I am proud of what I accomplished. All that said, I was ready to step away from my career and immerse myself in all the things I had post-poned during my work life.

"After a wonderful Mediterranean cruise with my husband, son, and daughter-in-law, I settled into my role as a retiree. I loved going to daily yoga, golfing during the week, and playing tennis at the club. I volunteered as a mentor for a national professional women's group. I enjoyed connecting with younger women and providing mentorship. Life was good. I had time to actually enjoy my coffee and sit on the patio. I had time to think.

"As I mentored young professional women, I was surprised that so many inequities I experienced still exist. Although legal and societal changes have helped, gender inequities still exist at work and at home for working career women. Having the time now to reflect on my career journey and hearing the younger women share their gender challenges triggered a latent sense of resentment. While focused on developing and then succeeding in my career, I never wanted to dwell on the negative--the barriers. I faced them and either barreled through or went around them. Clearly my male colleagues didn't experience these. I felt like one of those prairie dogs, always busy digging and then periodically popping up their heads above ground. When I popped my head up out of intensity of my career, I saw the big picture impact the inequities had on my stress level, personal time sacrifices, a very real glass ceiling, and less earning power.

"I can't recall who originated the line about Ginger

Rogers doing everything Fred Astaire did, but backwards and in heels. This summarized my growing resentment of how much harder I had to work in the same roles as my male counterparts. Three-quarters of my life is gone. This isn't a dress rehearsal. The fact that I spent so much of my life adapting to and navigating an inequitable, masculine workplace left me bitter. Let me be clear--I am grateful for all that my career provided. However, I couldn't escape my resentment.

"Why did I just accept that the CEO role in my last organization was out of limits for me? Why did I always feel like I had to put in more effort to prove my value? Why was I responsible for keeping the home run smoothly? Why did I have to feel like I constantly had to adapt to their world— their endless sports analogies, aggressive leadership styles, and devaluing of domestic responsibilities? Why was I put in a position to choose a career versus a larger family? My 'whys' continued for weeks. I snapped and barked at my husband. I wanted nothing to do with my former organization. I could feel the resentment physically manifest itself into a closing feeling in my throat. This wasn't how I pictured my retirement.

"Over a lengthy white wine lunch, a good friend patiently listened as I poured out decades of resentments. She suggested I do a few things: attend an upcoming women's empowerment retreat, begin journaling about my resentment, and turn my experiences into valuable coaching and mentoring for younger career women. Paging through my second journal, I see that I am in much better place today. My biggest healing continues to come from my mentorship of young women. Living somewhat vicariously through their career experiences, I have an empowering opportunity to change the script. What is my advice to other Boomer professional women who retire? Prepare yourself beyond the financial aspects."

Boomer Women Share Their Retirement Shock Stories

#2 Debbie

Debbie*, retired four years from her Silicon Valley executive position, encapsulates the identity shock retirement can bring.

"I traveled to Asia and India frequently, and this started to get old. These long trips and major time zone and dietary changes were hard on my body. I would arrive home on a Friday evening and fight jetlag (unsuccessfully) the entire weekend, then repeat the cycle the following week. It is not a good thing when the TSA agents know you by your first name. I had reached the C-Suite in the high-tech industry. I had nothing else to prove. I felt ready to have more time for my husband, my elderly parents, and myself. I had saved appropriately and worked with a financial planner. It seemed all was in place for me exit into retirement.

"The first six months were exhilarating. No alarm clocks and no smartphone incessantly buzzing. I visited my parents. My husband and I went on a cruise. I got involved in the Arts Council as a volunteer docent for the museum. I went through required volunteer training on how to greet guests, use the attendance counter, and count and record daily donations. I had to suppress a smile when the pedantic instructor asked me to demonstrating reconciling the donation monies and correctly entering the numbers into the ledger. I wanted to tell her that I had managed an $40 million budget and could handle this.

"As the year progressed, a vague malaise crept in. My beautiful home morphed from my nesting sanctuary in the early months of retirement to more of a source of isolation, devoid of stimulation. I had stopped our cleaning service, believing that it now that I was home, I could easily take on those duties. Well, it turns out I hate these duties. I had few playmates in my new-found freedom. My best friend was still employed. In just a few months I had run through my acquaintance list in scheduling lunches. I would watch the clock anxious for my husband's company after he arrived home from work. I had a physical exam and found some bone density issues, a sure sign of my aging. It was painful to speak to former co-workers and hear stories from my former world. On top of this, I had to plaster on a smile as I responded how much I loved retirement. I felt like the old me had vanished and I did not know who I was in this new world. My mother expressed her confusion as to why I was not more content now that I had stepped off my career treadmill. Finally, my husband told me to get some counseling or go back to work, because I was slowly sliding down into depression.

"I was embarrassed that I had to get help. Here I was, a super competent and confident executive. and I could not manage my own retirement transition. In working with a therapist and a coach, I came to see I was grieving the profound role work had in my life. It was also clear I needed to reinvent my new self. We worked on my values, created a purpose statement, and began identifying steps for me to meet my needs for challenge, connection, and accomplishment. Things got incrementally better. I found it validating that you called to interview me. I knew I could not have been the only one in retirement hell. However, few Boomer women are opening talking about the transition challenges. We need to have a clear vision for our retirement self and be open to support as we go through the retirement transition."

Tarnished Golden Years

Unprepared for the psychological aspects of retirement, most successful professionals, men or women, experience "retirement shock," resulting in an erosion of previously held identities. Gone are the symbols of power and status. Gone are the rewards and recognition. Gone are the daily stimuli of people and problem-solving. Of course, gone are the tangible perks of power. However, for Boomer professional women, we bring an additionally complex perspective to these transitional challenges. The fabric of our perspective is woven from inequities in a predominantly masculine work environment. Similarly, social values also placed a heavier burden of family responsibilities on us.

As we gain a new perspective in retirement, we more clearly see the reality of our pioneering professional experience. We made deep adaptations to the male system and innumerable sacrifices in an effort to prove ourselves; we pushed against systemic inequities. We tolerated and navigated these trials in an effort to create successful careers. Now that our careers are in the rearview mirror of our lives, resentment inevitably arises.

Despite these challenges, we carved out successful career identities. We relished the well-earned status and perks. There was no hesitation if someone asked us what we did for a living. In retirement, we no longer have our career identities nor the accompanying perks and power. As pioneering female professionals, we have no role female models to guide us. As accomplished women, adept at planning and managing, we were truly blindsided by the challenges of this transition. We also have difficulty sharing our experience, which is in direct contradiction to the Golden Years myth.

Preparing for the Psychology of Retirement

However, armed with knowledge and a roadmap, we *can* successfully move through this identity-challenging period of retirement. As Boomer professional women, we can leverage our collective activism, rooted in the Sixties and Seventies, to find our voice, work collaboratively, and navigate uncharted territory. We can create a pioneering, new retirement for Baby Boomer career women. Over 200 women interviewed for this book courageously shared their experiences and best practices for a psychologically successful retirement. In the chapters that follow, their insight is combined into a roadmap and practical strategies to help Boomer professional women reinvent a retirement that addresses our authentic selves.

TAKING TIME TO REFLECT:

1. Reflecting back on my career, what were the high points? What did this provide me beyond financial rewards?

2. Taking an honest inventory, what will I (or do I) miss the most about the perks and power of my former career? Any surprises here?

3. What will I say, in retirement, when asked, "What do you do?"

CHAPTER 5

"WHAT'S GOING ON?"

(Marvin Gaye)

Retirement Transition

The Big Event

The time has arrived for the "Big Event"--the obligatory retirement party. The room is filled with people, Happy Retirement banners, balloons, toasts and roasts, the buttercream sheet cake, gifts, and someone inevitably singing "Happy Trails to You." It can be simultaneously edifying and something to endure. It is hard to believe this day is finally here. Excitement and fear co-exist in the kaleidoscope of emotions enveloping the retiree. A retirement party is clearly a milestone marking the end of a career and the beginning of a new life stage. A celebratory rite of passage, the retirement party evokes a wide range of emotions from loss to liberation.

The next morning, we awaken "retired." The "Big Event" signifies our entry into the "no-work zone." As if by some

magical alchemy, our identity shifts overnight to that of being "retired." Almost immediately, we realize we don't know
how to retire. Now what? In reality, however, retirement is
not a discrete, overnight event; it is a process over a period of years. As with other major life transitions, such as
marriage, divorce, entering the workforce, or the death of
a loved one, these external events require internal adjustments. Transitions involve letting go, stepping into uncertainty, and re-emerging with a new sense of self.

As Boomer professional women, our investment in education and in our careers is a lifestyle, not merely a job.
For successful career professionals, retirement is one of
the most significant life transitions we will experience. The
complexity of this transition is compounded if retirement
was involuntary. Boomer professional women have little
understanding of the full range of adjustments required in
retirement. Past studies regarding retirement adjustment
did not include professional career women. This lack of information is another contributing factor to the retirement
"blindsiding" Boomer professional women. There is clearly
a dearth of research on Boomer professional women's retirement experience. However, as women gain greater critical mass in professional careers, we are beginning to see
more attention to the retirement issues we face. In fact, a
recent study interestingly finds that as more women have
entered into previous male-only professional roles, there is
increasing similarity in adjustments between male and female retirement transition. [73] It appears that as we climb up

the professional ladder, we are carrying some of the of the male work identity baggage.

However, retired professional women do report a greater loss of social status when they retire. One woman interviewed for a study on ageism and sexism indicated that upon retirement she lost the "Dr." title. Friends and former co-workers immediately began calling her "Mrs." rather than "Dr.""[74] It appears sexism and ageism followed these women into their retirement adjustment.

For the most part, we underestimate the magnitude of stress and adjustment associated with retirement. Retirement is listed as number 10 on the Holmes and Rahe Stress Scale of 43 stressful life events.[75] The top-rated adult life events listed in order of magnitude, are "death of a spouse, divorce, imprisonment" with retirement coming in as number 10 on this list of 43 life events. Decades of continuing studies validate the positive correlation between a high rating in life events rating and the potential for illness.

Many of us view retirement as an external change in our lives that we will need to accept and embrace over a relatively short period of time. In reality, given the impact of retirement on accomplished professionals, a deeper psychological shift and reinvention of our identity is required. In many ways, this is similar to the grieving process. When a close family member dies, there are common stages of grief, and ultimately the grieving person must reinvent themselves without their loved one. Whether a major life event of grief or retirement, both require psychological

reorientation and reinvention of self. However, if we understand, even anticipate, the magnitude of the transition and
the specific phases accompanying retirement, we are better equipped to successfully journey through this period in
our lives. As with any transition, the process of ending a life
phase and entering into a discovery eventually yields a new
beginning. Provided we lean into each phase, retirement
can be a creative time, providing opportunities for self-actualization and immense satisfaction.

Transitions 101

The words "change" and "transition" are often used
interchangeably. However, they have different meanings.
Change is a one-time, situational, tangible occurrence such
as relocating, changing jobs, getting married, or retiring.
Transition is how we internally process change. According
to William Bridges, authority on transitions, a transition is a
three-phase process where people gradually accept the de-
tails of the new situation and the changes that come with it.
[76] Of course, when faced with change, not all people all people embrace the necessary psychological adjustments that
create an internal shift. In a nutshell, transition is letting go
of how things were and embracing how they may become.

Earlier in this book, we explored retirement as a relatively new phenomenon beginning in the 20th century.
Retirement did not exist as a concept until the industrial
age shifted work from extended family farming to individualized factory work. For women, retirement is an even

more recent concept. Historically, retirement was the purview of men. Homemakers and "pink-collar" workers were not viewed as formally transitioning into retirement status in the same way as the male breadwinners. As the Boomer generation of women entered professional career roles, restrictive definitions of male-only retirement are becoming more and more obsolete. Whether stepping away from a professional career, entering bridge employment, adopting leisure activities, or some hybrid of the three, retirement is a major life transition. It is also uncharted territory for Boomer professional women.

In his seminal book *Managing Transitions*, William Bridges describes a psychological sequence through which we must move to successfully transition.[77] According to Bridges, all transitions begin with an ending. Whether a transition is perceived as positive or negative, they necessitate a letting go of something. In our case, retirement marks the end of our professional careers. Many of us are blindsided by the need to truly let go of our former professional identity. We literally need to say "goodbye," celebrating and grieving what once occupied thirty years of our lives.

Letting go can be particularly challenging as we move into Bridges' second stage of the "neutral zone." At this point, we have let go of the familiarity and certainty of our past career and are moving into what feels like a suspended state of uncertainty and chaos. In the "neutral zone," we wrestle with issues of identity. Coinciding with later adult life, retirement triggers a host of existential questions. If we are no longer a successful professional, then we ask: "Who am I? What is next? How will I spend this last chapter of my life? Were my career sacrifices worth it? What is my legacy?" and a host of other introspective inquiries. Bridges describes this period of inner examination like being "a shipwrecked sailor on some existential atoll." [78] Accustomed to being externally focused on our careers, we are often uncomfortable and unskilled with the self-exploration required to answer these questions.

It is understandable that we want to move quickly through the "neutral zone." If we ever jumped into another relationship soon after our previous one failed, it is likely we raced through our uncomfortable "neutral zone." We unwittingly hurtle into the arms of a rebound relationship, often rife with issues. Divorce courts are filled with people who sprinted through the "neutral zone." Panicked by the unexpected discomfort in this transition stage, many Boomer professional women quickly "unretire" and return to a career position. If we fasten our seatbelts and ride the neutral zone roller coaster, we find it is a highly generative transition stage. We find ourselves taking a personal inventory, questioning, reflecting, experimenting, and discovering our reinvented self. Our authentic values resurface. In many ways, we reconnect with the idealism of our youth. This authentic connection becomes our inner gyroscope as we design our new retirement lifestyle.

Having persevered through the neutral zone, we move to Bridges' final stage, known as "the new beginning." Here we moved from confusion to creativity and to a reinvented self. We said goodbye to our past identity and let it go. We did the heavy lifting work in the "neutral zone," resulting in a psychological shift and new behaviors. We step into a reinvented life with a sense of confidence and inner peace. Our retirement journey is comprised of endings, a neutral zone of uncertainty and discovery, and stepping into a new beginning.

Phases of Retirement

Viewing retirement as a transition process with distinct phases provides us with a common roadmap and language to better anticipate and understand our retirement experiences. Various models articulate sequential stages of the retirement process. In the 1970s, the US sociologist Robert Atchley proposed stages of the retirement process, which run counter to the common belief that retirement is an event. [79] Atchley acknowledges that individuals move through the stages in highly personalized ways of time and impact.

Achtley's model includes following six stages of retirement:

Phase 1 Pre-Retirement
Phase 2 Retirement
Phase 3 Disenchantment
Phase 4 Reorientation
Phase 5 Retirement Routine
Phase 6 Termination of Retirement

Atchley's model of the psychological stages of retirement is consistent with Bridges' model of transitions.

Achtley's stages include an ending (retirement), a neutral zone (disenchantment) and a new beginning (reorientation and retirement routine). Achtley added a termination step referencing return to work or death. Atchley's model is useful in its process focus, however, future adjustments to this model will be necessary. Rather than the historic "gold watch" and abrupt ending to work, Boomers are trailblazing a new "serial retirement." [80] Given our extended lifespans and higher levels of education, many of us are transitioning into retirement with bridge employment or even second and third careers. We may recycle through Atchley's stages multiple times in our decades of "retirement."

For most of us, the **"Phase 1 Pre-Retirement"** stage is synonymous with financial planning for retirement. For those of us whom retirement is voluntary, we have the "luxury" of time to emotionally process the concept of our retirement. Part of this Pre-Retirement period includes unexpected emotional shifts that begin to emerge. These shifts slowly distance us from the careers we worked so hard to create. Two to three years prior to our retirement, many of us begin experiencing decreasing satisfaction with the pillars of our career benefits. The accomplishments, promotions, power, perks, and material rewards begin to lose their luster. Harkening back to the hopes and dreams of our Baby Boomer youth, we experience an increasing yearning for more meaning, purpose, service, and fulfillment. We begin to shift from our laser-focused pursuit of career success and status to living a more authentic, values-based life.

During what we may now view as glacially paced corporate meetings, we find ourselves daydreaming more and more of an unstructured future. We envision no alarm clocks, time for ourselves, time to give back, and time for creative expression. We begin discussing "retiring someday" and sharing our dreams for retirement with others. The biggest outcome here is making the decision to retire. This represents a major life decision for us. We eventually select a date for our retirement. This is often followed with frequent discussions with Human Resources professionals. We are often busy ensuring our successor and departments are prepared for our departure.

Once again, if our retirement is involuntary, we are not afforded the much-needed rituals associated with this transition.

Assorted boxes in our arms, we exit our office for the last time. We are officially "retired." We are free to do whatever we want with our time. Gone are the high-pressured, structured, and time-constrained days of our career. We have entered **"Phase 2 Retirement"** stage, also known as the "honeymoon" period of retirement. This phase lasts between six and twelve months. This period is frequently described akin to a "sugar rush." [81] The freedom is exhilarating! We begin checking off items on our "bucket list." A smorgasbord of leisure activities and personal passions lies before us. Some women spend the first days of retirement taking long, recuperative afternoon naps. Others book travel with the novelty of not clearing their vacation time with a boss. Some actually exercise when they

have energy, versus the previous pre-dawn workout sessions. Others enroll in art classes or join book clubs. Some
seek out volunteer opportunities. Sometimes even the sim-
plest tasks bring a new freedom, such as food shopping on
a weekday morning, without Saturday checkout lines. Most
women cannot recall a previous time when they had this
much freedom to choose how to spend their time. Newly
retired women laughingly report savoring every new minute
of freedom. They typically dive into this new unconstrained
reality with the same zeal previously reserved for their career. Empty calendars frenetically fill up with an assortment
of leisure activities and pursuits of personal passion. This
period lasts about a year for most people.

For some the **third phase, "Disenchantment"** is a sud-
den, precipitous fall, and for others it is a slow drift. It can
last a couple years or even a decade, depending on the person's approach to inner discovery. Regardless, the day ar-
rives when we realize the retirement utopia we dreamed
about is more illusion than reality. A 2015 Mass Mutual
study comparing men's and women's retirement experience, found expectations for retirement tend to be exag-
gerated for many people, especially women, partly because
it is difficult for many people to envision what life in retirement will actually be like. [83] Women interviewed in this Mass
Mutual study had markedly higher expectations than men
for enjoying the social aspects of retirement and no longer
balancing professional careers with family responsibilities.

The initial excitement of a perpetual vacation loses

some of its luster. Continual travel for the next thirty years is not realistic. How many games of tennis can we play? Babysitting our beloved grandchildren simply does not provide the social and intellectual stimulation our former careers provided. From leading teams and garnering respect for our achievements, we find ourselves solitary hobbyists in our basements. [83] We are no longer viewed as vibrant, productive member of society. Interacting with our former co-workers often leaves us feeling margin. No longer an abstract concept, our mortality peers over the horizon. The later triggers our questioning our life purpose. We are experiencing the common phenomenon of the "retirement shock syndrome."

How could our early retirement "high" dissipate into this emotional ambush of grief, confusion, and assaults on our sense of identity? Although we planned carefully for our financial retirement, we never fully considered the disorienting social and psychological aspects that come with retirement. We were too busy focusing on our careers and perhaps families, keeping us from the necessary reflection, discovery, and planning for our life after our careers came to an end. Our financial portfolios are in good shape, but our retirement life portfolio is "underwater."

Compounding our sense of loss is shame. Society tells us retirement brings unprecedented opportunity, ushering in the Golden Years. However, this is not our reality. We are in the neutral zone of transition, marked by questioning, confusion, and dissatisfaction. We may even question our decision to retire. Most of the Boomer professional women interviewed indicated they were too embarrassed to share their feelings of loss and disenchantment. Long accustomed to success, feeling lost in the retirement abyss is unfamiliar and lonely for us. "People go through hell and never say a world about it. Cultural norms tell us retirement is the good life."[84]

Much as one loose stone can start an avalanche, initial examination of our decision to retire triggers additional questions about our life purpose. No longer successful professionals, often compounded by empty nests, we ask, "Who am I? What is next for me? Is this really the pot of gold at the end of my career rainbow? What will my marriage be like as my retirement continues? What is my legacy?"

Women who moved successfully moved through the **Disenchantment Phase** reported leaning into the discomfort and confusion. They acknowledged and processed their end-of-career grief. Tempted to return to the pace of their former careers, these women looked inward for what would truly make them happy. Women frequently stated they had always been expert at "doing," as their career success attested. However, during this Phase, they discovered they were inexperienced at just "being."

In the fourth phase, **"Reorientation,"** women interviewed took inventory of their values, desires, strengths, and potential outlets for each of these. They spent time in reflection and introspection, discovering who they authentically wanted to become in this next stage of their lives. They were also willing to experiment with different interests and outlets. Finally, the most successful women had the courage to reach out to other Boomer professional women struggling with the same retirement adjustment issues. With the hindsight of successfully designing their retirement life, these women described the months and even years in this phase as ultimately one of the most creative and self-fulfilling times of their lives.

The fifth phase, **"Routine Retirement,"** describes a period of acceptance, stability, and comfort with our customized retirement lifestyles. We are living our values and passion-based retirement lifestyle playbook. Similar to other life transitions, we have moved through turbulence to clear air. This is especially evident in the early part of our careers. For many of us, there were uncertain and circuitous routes to settling in on a solid career path. Once the path was clear, we plugged ourselves into a familiar and primarily satisfying, routine work lifestyle. Reaching the **"Routine Retirement Phase"** is much the same. For the women interviewed, "routine" retirement manifested in a myriad of lifestyles--everything from meaningful volunteering, entrepreneurial ventures, part-time employment, academic studies, competitive sports activities, and artistic explorations to hands-on grandparenting. Although many different retirement playbooks were created, all of these women invested time and emotion to design a highly satisfying retirement lifestyle.

Achtley's final Phase, **"Termination of Retirement,"** is characterized by death or a return to career employment. The first prospect, although a reality, is rather depressing. I am happy to say that the over 200 women I interviewed are healthy and very much still here. Seven women did choose to return to their professional careers. Their decisions were attributed to reactions to the discomfort of the "Disenchantment Phase," a dramatic change in financial security, and a truly well-thought-out decision.

Unsuspecting Pioneers

The Boomer professional women interviewed repeatedly shared being unprepared for the roller-coaster ride of adjusting to their retirement. They described exhilarating heights in the early phases. This was followed by heart-pounding plunges into the depths of dissatisfaction. Through self-discovery and experimentation, they shared climbing back to levels of hopefulness and finally to exiting the roller coaster ride of retirement transition. Their key observation was being unprepared for this ride. Highly competent in their former professional careers, these women were truly perplexed as to why they never considered planning beyond the financial aspects of their retirement. They were also frustrated that no one, including their financial advisors, forewarned them. Becoming gender pioneers once again was not on their radar.

Boomer Professional Women
Share Their Transition Experiences

#1 Diane

Diane*, a Senior Vice-President of Business Development for a Fortune 100 financial services company, describes her

EMPTY NEST, EMPTY DESK, WHAT'S NEXT?

"ride" as one of the most profound periods of transitions in her life. She typifies Boomer professional women who attempt to insulate themselves from the discomfort of the neutral zone and disenchantment phase with emotionally distracting busyness.

"Once I made up my mind to step out of the 'rat race,' I couldn't wait until my official retirement day. I had worked with a financial advisor for years. I trusted her completely and she understood my tolerance for risk. I remember her 'talking me off the ledge' when the economy tanked in 2008. As the economy moved out of that mess, I was confident I did have enough retirement funds to live comfortably. Note I said comfortably, not extravagantly. My financial advisor always smiles when I qualify my retirement financial lifestyle. The fact is that I have quite a sizable retirement portfolio.

"Yes, they had a retirement party for me. It was at a local hotel. As part of my retirement 'roast.' people stepped up to the podium and recounted funny and often embarrassing stories. A couple people on my team did a skit representing me in retirement. They dressed in a gray wig, sat in a rocking chair, and had me watching one of those banal game shows on television. Initially I laughed along with everyone. However, deep inside this 'Grandma Moses' image was unsettling. This inactive, old person was not my image of my future self in retirement.

"During the first few weeks of retirement, I vacillated between feeling ecstatic and feeling guilty. There were some days when I felt like I was truant from school. I felt like somehow I was playing hooky from my real, productive life. I was surprised that I felt guilty. I began traveling a great deal. I signed up for ballroom dancing. I joined a tennis league. I joined a book club.

I even signed up for a series of cooking classes. I wanted to just keep busy, busy, busy.

"When not joining a league, club, or in a class, I focused on things I wanted to do around the house. For decades, my clothes closet looked as if an Improvised Explosive Device (IED) had exploded in its midst. I finally had the time to take on a major closet reorganizing project. My goal was to downsize and create a minimalist approach to my wardrobe. I wanted to put an end to my familiar morning archeological dig trying to locate a particular article of clothing. In a way, my cluttered closet represented the personal time challenges and chaos of my thirty-seven-year career of nonstop traveling and sixty-hour workweeks. I spent days sorting my clothes into large piles of keep, discard, or donate. I found duplicate items still containing the retail tags. I shook my head at the amount of retail therapy damage I had done over the years. I made almost daily trips to the local container and organization store. I felt pride when I ferreted out new organizational gadgets. How did I ever live without tiered hangers or vacuum -sealed space saver bags? At the end of the month, my reorganization project was complete. I had transformed my closet.

"A few days later, I was catching up with a former work colleague. She inquired about what I was doing. I went into a detailed recounting of my closet reorganization project. I launched into the benefits of the 'As Seen on TV Magic Hangers'. I suddenly could hear myself speaking and felt embarrassed. How pathetic. Is this why I retired? I could practically hear the sonic boom of the 'retirement shock waves' that hit me. I felt like somewhere between installing the closet storage system and innumerous trips to Goodwill, I lost my old self. I knew at that moment there would never be enough closets to replace the void left when I gave up my former executive identity.

"For the first time in my life, I felt like a has-been, old, and marginal. I planned more trips, but these only temporarily assuaged my growing dissatisfaction and even depression. My lunches with former co-workers became torturous as they talked about the world I left behind. I floated in this private, unhappy cloud for about eighteen months. One day, while paging through the AARP Magazine, I focused in on an article about the challenges executives experience in retirement. There is a need to let go and reinvent your life as a retiree. This was eye-opening, as it put words to my nebulous dissatisfaction.

"I did more research and sought out a professional life coach who focused on retirement. We worked on who I wanted to become in this post-career phase of my life. Fast forward to today—more than three years since my retirement. I am in a good place today. My life involves part-time consulting with a local entrepreneur support network in my city, traveling, and just plain relaxing. For me, I needed the stimulation of work, but just not on my former scale of stress and responsibility. On average, I work about fifteen hours per week, but I have tremendous flexibility to set my own schedule.

"In retrospect, I was unprepared for the emotional and psychological challenges that come with retirement. I regret not having a lifestyle plan. My real priority should have been transforming myself not my closet. Ha. I hope my story helps someone else. Life is too short to squander it being unhappy."

Diane's* story is a good example of our natural bias for action versus exploring uncomfortable emotions. This talent for implementation and execution served us well during our careers. However, it can be a liability in the neutral zone of retirement transition. The tectonic plates of our identities shift as we move through our retirement transitions. Just as the earth's shifting plates redistribute the earth's surface, retirement reorganizes our sense of self. Rather than sprint through these hot zone fault lines, we are better served spending the time needed to discover who we want to become in this next life chapter.

Boomer Professional Women
Share Their Transition Experiences

#2 Robin

Robin*, a former executive administrator for a prestigious university, shared that when the honeymoon stage of her retirement came to an end, she experienced a myriad of surprising emotions. One of her predominant emotions was grief.

"About a year into my retirement, I started to feel restless. I was doing everything I always wanted to do that my former career prevented. I was exercising daily and had lost fifteen pounds. I could pick up and travel whenever the whim struck me. I volunteered at church. I bought a kiln and began making pottery again. It all sounds great—right? I mean, it was a heck of a lot better than late-night conference calls and trustee presentations that rivaled the Spanish Inquisition! However, I walked around with a growing sense of sadness and emptiness. What was wrong with me?

"The only other time I felt something similar to this was when my dad passed away. I spent that first year after his death in a cloud of grief. I went through the motions of life, but at my core I felt desolate. A concerned, good friend gave me a book on the journey of grief. After a few months collecting dust on my coffee table, I finally read the book. The emotions of grief presented in the book articulated the arc of my emotions. My first revelation was that I wasn't crazy. My emotions were normal. I now had a better understanding of what I was feeling and a language to describe my experiences. This was a turning point.

"I never expected to feel grief and loss associated with retirement. I had looked forward to retirement. It was my choice and my timing. However, there was no denying that I was feeling grief. I wasn't processing these feelings of loss.

I had put enormous energy into my career for over thirty years. When asked what I did for a living, I smoothly described myself as an 'executive in higher education'. I liked the interest and respect my role garnered from others. I enjoyed speaking at prestigious conferences. I enjoyed the daily interaction with bright, accomplished colleagues. I enjoyed the ever-present problem- solving. I enjoyed the recognition of achievements. Although this may seem shallow, I even enjoyed my designated parking spot.

"Once I retired, I had only a jumble of words to describe what I did now. I either resuscitated my former role explaining what I used to do, or I sounded like vacuous to-do list of leisure activities. I am embarrassed to admit I deeply missed my former role. Here I am with a Ph.D. and I had no clue that emotions of loss would surface so strongly when I retired. I mean, I had no clue and no preparation. Thinking back to my previous experience with loss and grief, I knew I had a starting point. I wrote about what I was feeling in what became a well-worn journal. I even went through the ritual of celebrating my past career and saying a formal goodbye to this period in my life. Once I grieved, I was ready to step into my retirement life.

"As the grief lifted, I became involved in a virtual Boomer women's retirement group. From these women, just like me, I learned various ways to recreate some of the things I was missing that were formerly provided by my career. I added a book club and a retired university women's group to my retirement lifestyle portfolio. This met my need for collegiality with bright, educated professional women. I stepped into a volunteer leadership role at my church, providing me with problem-solving challenges and more opportunity for achievement. My biggest lesson to share with others is to expect some grief over the loss of your former identity. After all, we worked hard to obtain these identities and they were with us for decades. Also, you can run but you can't hide from emotions. The only way out of the sadness is through it."

Both Diane* and Robin* represent many Boomer professional women who were unprepared for the psychological adjustments inherent in retirement. Many of us erroneously view retirement as an event. We view retirement as the farewell party event and then expect to wake up magically transitioned into our new retirement identity. In reality, retirement is a major life transition and consists of a phased adjustment process. Key to a successful retirement adjustment is a journey inward to perhaps grieve the ending of our career and to connect what will authentically create fulfillment in this next life stage. The women who reported a high level of retirement satisfaction were the women who journeyed through each phase of the retirement process to ultimately arrive at the "Routine Retirement" phase. The following chapters synthesize the many transition best practices they generously shared. Common themes emerged. These are organized into a repeatable process to help guide other Boomer professional women considering retirement or currently in their retirement journey.

TAKING TIME TO REFLECT:

1. Where am I in Atchley's psychological stages of retirement? In this stage, what has been challenging for me? Where have I found success in this stage?

2. If asked how my retirement is going, how would I respond?

3. On a scale from one (low) to ten (high), how would I rate my preparation for the psychological adjustments of retirement? Why?

CHAPTER 6

"BRIDGE OVER TROUBLED WATER"

(Simon and Garfunkel)

A Roadmap for Redefining Our Retirement

Finally, a Map!

Whenever Boomer professional women discussed the wonders of retirement, I began to notice a similar "Golden Years" script: "Oh, I love retirement. It is great. No clocks. No stress." I also could not help but notice that their smiles often looked forced. The greater reality is that high-achieving professional women are generally not comfortable in sharing their retirement "letdown." First of all, we are used to success, and retirement dissatisfaction borders closely with perceived failure. Discussing our unhappiness is akin to admitting we made a serious miscalculation with our decision to retire. Society clearly views retirement as a reward and life pinnacle for all our hard work. Marketing messages reaffirm this. We often conclude that something must be wrong with us, if we don't fully embrace retirement. Finally, there is the isolation that often accompanies retirement, limiting opportunities to garner support.

However, as I shared my own experience and those of others, more and more women opened up. Disingenuous facades crumbed. Freed from our emotional forgery, we begin to share our genuine experience and emotions. We also begin to share strategies that have helped us. From this fertile field of best practices, I created the "Reinventing Boomer Retirement Roadmap©" process designed to provide insight, design, direction, and action resulting in a truly satisfying retirement. See **Figure 1** at the end of this Chapter. As women retirement pioneers, we now have the missing roadmap. Through my interviews, the myriad of best practices aligned around the themes represented in the five-step "Reinventing Boomer Retirement Roadmap©." Each step contains tools and exercises to positively move us forward through the neutral zone of retirement transition. Whether we are planning to retire or currently retired, this roadmap enhances our retirement journey.

Step 1 of the process begins with a "READINESS Reality Check," assessing readiness for retirement on a number life-planning aspects. In Step 1 we identify the life plan issues with the greatest potential to derail our retirement satisfaction. In addition, it explores how to leverage strengths and mitigate challenges experienced with past transitions.

Step 2, "Finding Your WHY," explores our authentic selves, core values, life purpose, and legacy. The confluence of aging and retirement heighten our sense of mortality and search for meaning in our lives. Why were we here? What is our life purpose? This is our last chance to make our life mission a reality. In Step 2, powerful questions stimulate an inner journey to our core "Why." Tools and exercises guide us through this process to inner clarity.

With insight gained in Step 2, we move to creating a bold life design based on our "Why." In Step 3, "So, What DO you <u>Really</u> Want?" we literally map out a holistic vision for our lives. This is our blueprint for how we plan to spend our newly acquired 2,000 hours of free time per year (8 hours/day X 5 days X 50 weeks = 2,000). Through unique tools and exercises, we formulate the "What" to our "Why."

In Step 4, "Do You Have the RIGHT STUFF?" we assess what it will take internally and externally to bring our life vision to fruition. Using customized tools, we first identify the skills, experiences, and mindset required by our vision. Then we implement 360-degree feedback and self-assessment of the skills, experiences, and mindset required. This assessment provides us with areas to leverage, gaps to close, and identifies needed resources and support.

Then it is time to put our insight, design, and assessment work into action in Step 5, "Making It Happen." Using a comprehensive visual planning tool, we map out our action plan. We build in strategies for milestone accountability and metrics for success.

In the remaining chapters, we will explore each Step in the "Reinventing Boomer Retirement Roadmap©" in greater detail. We will understand and work with the tools, templates, question guides and maps associated with each Step. In addition, from retired Boomer professional women, we will learn about real-world application and best practices of these resources.

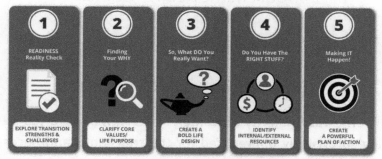

Figure 1

CHAPTER 7

"I CAN SEE CLEARLY NOW"

(Johnny Nash)

Retirement Reality Check

Exploring the Reality Check Tools

The vast majority of women I interviewed reported being surprisingly unprepared for the transitions and necessary adjustments retirement presents. In their professional careers, these women regularly employed audits, analysis, and action planning to manage their areas of responsibility. Yet, like so many of us, they abandoned these proven and familiar practices when addressing their retirement. Most women were incredulous regarding their lack of systematic analysis and planning for the next 20-30 years of their retirement lives. The most common feelings described were those of being "blindsided" and feeling "incompetent" when it came to their retirement planning. We need to give ourselves a break. After all, we are more accustomed to the external focus of work than the internal focus of assessing our emotions, values, and beliefs.

An important first step in any planning includes assessing our current situation. In Boomer 1960s slang, this is known as a "reality check." The first step in the **Retirement Roadmap**© is literally a "Readiness Reality Check". We identify strengths to leverage and gaps to close and incorporate these into our Retirement Life Plan. The tools in this first step of the **Reinventing Boomer Retirement Roadmap**© help us to holistically assess our readiness for retirement, identify gaps, and incorporate strategies to close these gaps and/or leverage our strengths in our Retirement Life Plan. In essence, this is our retirement "reality check."

Although we may have created a solid financial portfolio, this does not address the other aspects of life that provide balance, meaning, and fulfillment. These include Life Purpose, Health, Relationships, Community Engagement, Leisure, and Social Life. The diagnostic tool, *Retirement Readiness Questionnaire*©*, (Figure 2),* provides questions designed to identify our current satisfaction with each of these pillars of a balanced and fulfilled life. This tool gives us a holistic snapshot of areas to leverage and areas for development indicating our readiness for a balanced retirement lifestyle. The **Wheel of Readiness**©, **Figure 3**, graphically records the results from the *Retirement Readiness Questionnaire*©.

RETIREMENT READINESS DIAGNOSTIC QUESTIONNAIRE©

INSTRUCTIONS: Select the response that most accurately describes your level of agreement with the statement. In the blank space to the left of each question, place the number corresponding to your selection. Example:

1. I am confident my retirement will be the best time of my life

1. Strongly Disagree	2. Disagree	3. Agree	4. Strongly Agree
☐	☐	☒	☐

1. I can easily articulate my life purpose.

1. Strongly Disagree	2. Disagree	3. Agree	4. Strongly Agree
☐	☐	☐	☐

2. I share my dreams and fears about retirement with my spouse/partner/significant person.

1. Strongly Disagree	2. Disagree	3. Agree	4. Strongly Agree
☐	☐	☐	☐

3. I spend 5+ hours per month serving my community with my skills and talents.

1. Strongly Disagree	2. Disagree	3. Agree	4. Strongly Agree
☐	☐	☐	☐

4. I am connected to events in our community.

1. Strongly Disagree	2. Disagree	3. Agree	4. Strongly Agree
☐	☐	☐	☐

6. I typically spend 3 + hours per week engaged in hobby activities.

1. Strongly Disagree	2. Disagree	3. Agree	4. Strongly Agree
☐	☐	☐	☐

7. I leverage expert financial retirement advisory resources.

1. Strongly Disagree	2. Disagree	3. Agree	4. Strongly Agree
☐	☐	☐	☐

8. I have multiple non-work opportunities for cognitive enrichment.

1. Strongly Disagree	2. Disagree	3. Agree	4. Strongly Agree
☐	☐	☐	☐

9. I live a majority of life in alignment with my values..

1. Strongly Disagree	2. Disagree	3. Agree	4. Strongly Agree
☐	☐	☐	☐

Dr. Rita Smith

Figure 2

10. I regularly see healthcare professionals for preventative health care.

1. Strongly Disagree	2. Disagree	3. Agree	4. Strongly Agree
☐	☐	☐	☐

11. I am connected with a spiritual community.

1. Strongly Disagree	2. Disagree	3. Agree	4. Strongly Agree
☐	☐	☐	☐

12. I exercise 30 minutes 3-5 times per week.

1. Strongly Disagree	2. Disagree	3. Agree	4. Strongly Agree
☐	☐	☐	☐

13. I have a balanced mix of friends from work and outside of work.

1. Strongly Disagree	2. Disagree	3. Agree	4. Strongly Agree
☐	☐	☐	☐

14. I am satisfied with the amount of leisure time I spend with my family.

1. Strongly Disagree	2. Disagree	3. Agree	4. Strongly Agree
☐	☐	☐	☐

15. I can easily identify new hobbies/leisure activities I will explore in retirement.

1. Strongly Disagree	2. Disagree	3. Agree	4. Strongly Agree
☐	☐	☐	☐

16. I have a diverse network of people in my life.

1. Strongly Disagree	2. Disagree	3. Agree	4. Strongly Agree
☐	☐	☐	☐

17. I am satisfied with my level of physical fitness.

1. Strongly Disagree	2. Disagree	3. Agree	4. Strongly Agree
☐	☐	☐	☐

18. I diligently saved funds for my retirement lifestyle.

1. Strongly Disagree	2. Disagree	3. Agree	4. Strongly Agree
☐	☐	☐	☐

19. I can easily make time for my friends.

1. Strongly Disagree	2. Disagree	3. Agree	4. Strongly Agree
☐	☐	☐	☐

Dr. Rita Smith

Figure 2

20. I regularly seek comfort in spiritual practices during times of uncertainty.

1. Strongly Disagree   2. Disagree   3. Agree   4. Strongly Agree

☐   ☐   ☐   ☐

21. I have a solid plan in place to ensure my retirement aligns with my inner desires.

1. Strongly Disagree   2. Disagree   3. Agree   4. Strongly Agree

☐   ☐   ☐   ☐

22. I can easily identify volunteer activities with which to engage.

1. Strongly Disagree   2. Disagree   3. Agree   4. Strongly Agree

☐   ☐   ☐   ☐

23. I consistently create time and space for my spiritual journey.

1. Strongly Disagree   2. Disagree   3. Agree   4. Strongly Agree

☐   ☐   ☐   ☐

24. I am actively connected to a hobby/leisure community.

1. Strongly Disagree   2. Disagree   3. Agree   4. Strongly Agree

☐   ☐   ☐   ☐

25. I am satisfied with my financial portfolio.

1. Strongly Disagree   2. Disagree   3. Agree   4. Strongly Agree

☐   ☐   ☐   ☐

Dr. Rita Smith

Figure 2

RETIREMENT READINESS DIAGNOSTIC QUESTIONNAIRE© SCORING

INSTRUCTIONS: Place the numeric score corresponding to each question in the appropriate boxes below. Then total each box. Example:

COMMUNITY ENGAGEMENT
3. 2
5. 1
22. 4
Total =

CLEAR LIFE PURPOSE
1. _____
8. _____
20. _____
Total = _____

COMMUNITY ENGAGEMENT
3. _____
4. _____
21. _____
Total = _____

FAMILY/ RELATIONSHIPS
2. _____
13. _____
18. _____
Total = _____

FINANCIAL
6. _____
17. _____
23. _____
Total = _____

HOBBY/LEISURE
5. _____
7. _____
14. _____
Total = _____

PHYSICAL HEALTH
9. _____
11. _____
16. _____
Total = _____

SPIRITUAL DEVELOPMENT
10. _____
19. _____
22. _____
Total = _____

SOCIAL LIFE BEYOND WORK
12. _____
15. _____
21. _____
Total = _____

Figure 2

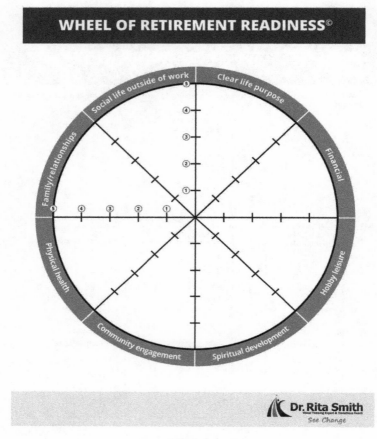

Figure 3

The **_Work: Power and Perks_ (Figure 4)** tool takes us beyond the euphoria of no alarm clocks and free time to help us understand the void not working creates in our lives. We identify the intangible rewards our career provided. We then assess the value of each and the difficulty level to replace these in our lives.

For high-achieving, successful professionals the need for intangibles such as achievement, productivity, and recognition do not go away just because we are retired.

WORK: POWER & PERKS, ITS ABOUT MORE THAN JUST THE MONEY©

INSTRUCTIONS:
While it is often easy to list characteristics of work we are happy to leave, such as early alarm clocks and the volume of meetings, it is more difficult to identify what we will lose. In the blank spaces, list what you anticipate losing or have lost due to retirement. Rank the value to you using the ratings Hi, Med. Or Lo. Then, using the same rating scale, rate how difficult it is to replace this loss. Circle your top 3 areas containing both high value and corresponding high difficulty to replace. This reality check about power, perks and other areas of satisfaction gained from work and the difficulty or ease of replacing will be helpful as you create your reinventing retirement plan.

	VALUE	DIFFICULTY TO REPLACE		VALUE	DIFFICULTY TO REPLACE

Figure 4

The final tool of our Retirement Reality Check process is the **Timeline of Our Life's Key Transitions (Figure 5).** This exercise asks us to reflect on key life transitions in our past.

We then assess the ease or difficulty of these transitions on an adjustment continuum. The final step is to look for behavioral and attitudinal patterns, areas of strength to leverage, and areas requiring further development and support as we journey through our retirement transition.

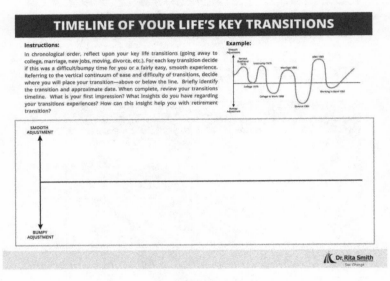

Figure 5

This chapter concludes with reflective questions, tying together our observations and insight from our work with the first step, *Retirement Reality Check.* We will incorporate these tools and reflective insights into the later creation of our Retirement Life Plan. In addition to the Reinventing Boomer Retirement Roadmap Tools appearing in this chapter, they are also included in the Tools section of this book.

A Closer Look at the Pillars of a Balanced Life

Life purpose provides central motivation to our lives. It involves using our best qualities, and signature talents and passions in service of something bigger than ourselves. Knowing our unique reason "why we are here" guides our decisions, behavior, goals, direction, and ultimately creates meaning in our lives. In retirement, we have the opportunity to return to the world for the better. As we grew older and shifted our focus to career and family, many of us put our "change the world" life purpose on hold. We are now gifted with a second chance to revisit a greater sense of purpose to our lives. As humans, we are psychologically wired to find purpose and meaning in our lives. A 2014 Psychological Science study cited a strong link between life purpose in older adults and increased life expectancy. [85] Discovering our life purpose is foundational to a fulfilled retirement.

Good health is so critical to our living a full retirement experience over the next 20-30 years. Some of us are able to squeeze fitness, mindful eating, and stress management into our career lifestyles, but many of us fall short due to the lack of discretionary time. Retirees report the number one ingredient for happy retirement, by a significant margin, is good health. Good health was 23 points higher than the next rated ingredient for happiness: financial security. [86]

A third pillar of balanced retirement is **relationships.** For this discussion, relationships refers to family. Retirement will create change in family relationships. Retirement forces couples to spend more time together than ever before.

Cracks in the relationship tend to grow to deep crevasses. If one spouse retires prior to the other, this also causes strain.

Interestingly, professional career women initiative over two-thirds of divorce proceedings in couples over age fifty.[87] Retirement can also be a time to recapture weakened connections caused after years of careers competing for family time.

Finally, most retirees have adult children, and negotiating relationship boundaries and other issues such as caretaking of grandchildren will arise. Assessing the current state of our familial relationships helps us to identify and possibly pre-empt or repair potential issues.

Community engagement primarily refers to volunteering. As Boomer professional women, we are highly educated and possess valuable skillsets. In retirement, we have opportunity to use these assets to provide value for others. David Eisner, CEO of the Corporation for National and Community Service, promotes and develops volunteer opportunities for older Americans. He observes, "Boomers came of age when Kennedy famously asked what they could do for their country, and that sense of idealism remains in place today. Our research shows many Boomers are motivated to make a meaningful difference.[88] In addition, medical studies repeatedly tout the many physical and mental benefits of volunteering for the retiree. A 2009, study by researchers at the John Hopkins Bloomberg School of Public Health points to an increase in the maintenance of the brain's executive functions of volunteers compared to non-volunteers.[89]

The balanced life pillar of **Leisure** refers to how we use our newfound discretionary time. For the first time since early childhood, we have control over how we chose to spend our free time. We may choose passive, active, group or individual ways to relax or recreate. Researchers emphasize the need for physical activity as part of our leisure activities. Regular physical activity for adults over forty is correlated to an increased life span of four years.[90] Again, assessing where we are now will help enrich our retirement planning.

The final balanced life pillar is **Social Life,** primarily focusing on friendships. An important aspect of a successful retirement life is staying connected to others. We often underestimate the role our co-workers played in our "social life" during our working years. A Stanford Center for Longevity Study conducted in 2017, found socially isolated adults face health risks comparable to smokers.[91] That is quite a sobering observation on the human need for social connection.

Once you complete and score the **Retirement Readiness Diagnostic Questionnaire**, populate your scores on the Retirement Readiness Wheel. This Wheel provides a visual snapshot of our current satisfaction level in the various categories comprising a balanced life. Using the wheel metaphor, is our Wheel well rounded, or are we in for a bumpy ride?

A Client's Journey Through Step One: Retirement Readiness Check

After my client Amy*, a public relations Vice President, completed her Retirement Readiness Wheel, she shared surprise and some shame in how out-of-balance her life had become.

"For decades, my focus was growing my career. I lost the perspective to see how other aspects of my life were neglected. The Wheel exercise was a wake-up call for me. I regret I did not have this insight a few years back. But then would I have addressed the gaps without the urgency and reality of my upcoming retirement? Maybe I could have selected a few priority things to work on.

"I do feel gratitude that I can begin closing some of these gaps before I retire next year. Outside of work, my life is very limited. Without this outside engagement and connection, I can just imagine myself pacing the house and looking out the window in my retirement. That is not the picture I want to envision for myself!"

Rather than move into an action-oriented executive mode and immediately jump into a variety of community and religious groups to close the gaps, I recommended Amy work through the entire Reinventing Boomer Retirement process. This would ensure her goals and activities are aligned with her core values, passions, and life purpose.

Completing the Work: Power & Perks exercise also contributed to Amy's clarity. For Amy, it became clear that she would sorely miss opportunities for accomplishment and collegiality. Amy observed, "I've always been energized by achieving. I was the straight-A student, I completed my doctoral dissertation in record time, and really loved a tough work challenge. There is nothing like the satisfaction of successfully tackling an important work issue. My achievements garnered me recognition and of course, upward career progression. I am not a solo act, though. I get my energy from people. My best career memories are working with teams of people. My work colleagues became my work family. I can't imagine myself getting this level of achievement and collegial satisfaction in solo leisure activities."

The next Retirement Reality Check tool asks us to reflect on how we handled previous transitions in our lives. Reflecting back on key transitions in our past, we rate the ease or difficulty in our adjustment to these transitions. The objective here is to look for the transition that went smoothly--or conversely, that were difficult. In addition, patterns may emerge that highlight the types of transitions that trigger a certain adjustment response. The final step is to identify what worked and did not work in both the smooth and bumpy transitions. For Amy, her smoothest transitions involved relationships. When I asked her why she believed this to be true, she indicated she has a strong network with whom to share her feelings. "I have a few friends that I can call any time of the day or night and cry on their shoulders. No matter how low I felt after a break-up or my divorce, I could lean on this circle of friends. I also found journaling to be a good outlet for me."

When asked the same question regarding her bumpy adjustment transitions, Amy responded, "There is definitely a pattern of school and work with my bumpier adjustments. I feel my achievement identity is very tied up in both of these arenas. Asking for support feels like an admission that I am a failure. I kept a lot of my fears, depression, and even anxiety mostly to myself. I viewed work requiring me to be a strong woman professional. No whining. No crying, just suck it up. Letting others see my vulnerability is too threatening for me. That is why my working with you on reinventing my retirement is out-of-character. One of my friends pushed me to start thinking about and planning for my retirement. She won her case by telling me that she has watched me lose myself with my career, and she is concerned that I will be stepping into a deep void when I retire. Something deep inside me whispered that she is right."

Over the next 180 days, Amy continued to work the remaining five steps in the Reinventing Boomer Retirement Roadmap© using the tools introduced in the chapters that follow.

A collection of Powerful Questions closes this Retirement Readiness Reality Check step. The questions synthesize the exercises and are designed to cull insight, provoke honest assessment, create a sense of urgency, and motivate action.

After years in successful professional roles, we are biased toward action. Introspection via quiet reflection time is an anathema. However, based on studies and empirical evidence, key thought leaders view reflection as a prerequisite to self-growth. Chris Argyris, well-known Harvard professor, aptly stated, "Without self-awareness, you cannot understand your strengths and weaknesses, your 'super powers' versus your 'kryptonite.'"[92] In addition, Peter Drucker, largely considered the father of modern management, emphasized, "From the quiet reflection will come more effective action."[93] Facing the longest unstructured period and likewise our last life stage, we need to have intimate knowledge of our "super powers" and "kryptonite" from which we can create a truly amazing retirement life plan.

CHAPTER 8

"LIGHT MY FIRE"

(The Doors)

Finding Our Why

Meaning and Purpose in Our Lives

The retirement transition represents the end of a career. This is a big ending. After all, we invested time and money in our professional educations. We adapted ourselves to a male workplace. We worked long hours. We logged many airline miles crisscrossing the globe. For decades, we identified with a career role and now it no longer fits. Any transition, such as retirement, compels us to reflect back and reflect forward. When we retire, we become increasingly aware of entering the "last chapter" of our lives and even our own mortality. Facing our mortality triggers many emotions. Within this emotional milieu are both the pain of loss and regret and the promise of making our last years meaningful.

The need for purpose is one of the definitive characteristics that distinguish human beings from other species.

We crave purpose. It is fundamental to our living a satisfying life.

A common theme in the work of sociologists and psychologists is our need to make our life count. One such psychologist is Erik Erikson. In the 1950s, Erikson created an Eight Stage Model of Human Development. Each stage is triggered by a transition and describes both the negative and positive attitudes and behavior choices typical of each stage. Erikson's Seventh State is Generativity versus Stagnation. Basically, Erikson is saying that as we reach our middle years and beyond, we have a natural desire and need for purpose to contribute to the betterment of people beyond ourselves. [94] The choice is ours to make.

Life purpose comes from within. It encompasses our values, passions and talents. For many years our life purpose was inseparable from our intense career focus. As stated above, retirement is a catalyst for reflection. Perhaps for the first time in our lives, we ask ourselves, "Did my life matter?" We are forces to acknowledge that the majority of our lives are behind us. One of the requirements of unlocking our life purpose is to come face-to-face with our own mortality. [95] Calculating the days potentially left in your life is a sobering activity. Simply multiply your current age X 365 days/year and then subtract this number from 30,000 days, the average life expectancy.[96] We have a finite number of days ahead in which to make our being here has meaning— literally outliving ourselves. Once we process the immense concept of our own mortality, we can use this as a springboard for making each day count.

The effort to unlock our life purpose is more than an exercise in self-actualization. Research points to the health benefits of having a clear life purpose. In Dan Buettner's study of "Blue Zones (communities in the world in which people are more likely to live past 100 years), one of key factors most centenarians share was having a strong sense of purpose. [97] Another study in 2008 found that a lower level of purpose in Japanese men was associated with earlier death and cardiovascular disease. More research in this area showed that "purpose is a possible protective factor against near-future myocardial infarction among those with coronary heart disease. [98] In studying elderly subjects, Dr. Patricia Boyle, a neuropsychologist with the Rush Alzheimer's Disease Center, found that people with a strong sense of life purpose were 2.4 times less likely to develop Alzheimer's disease than those with a low sense of life purpose. Those with a strong life purpose were also less likely to develop mobility disabilities.[99]

Additionally, in 2009, MetLife Mature Market Institute's conducted research measurably linking physical and emotional health benefits to having a life purpose. [100] This research showed that having a clear life purpose was the differentiator to those identified living the Good Life. Richard Leider defines the Good Life as being more than material wealth and physical comfort, but also "living in the place your belong, with the people you love, while doing the right work on purpose." [101] They were then asked to rate the extent to which they felt they are living the "Good Life" and this was correlated to their identification of having a clear life purpose. For those living the "Good Life," 84% had a clear life purpose versus 33% of those not living the "Good Life." [102] Research continues in moving the philosophical concept of having "a life purpose" to an imperative for wellbeing.

In the sections that follow, we will examine the components of life purpose: values, passion and talents. Increasing our understanding of these components and getting clear on our own values, passion and talents will result in creating version 1.0 of our life purpose statement.

Core Values

Our personal values are an expression of what is most important to us. They influence our decisions and behaviors. They are guiding principles functioning as our personal compass. The combination of values we regard as highest priority is unique and subjective to each of us. Akin to our fingerprints, we each have a set of core values of which we prioritize. We may share a few personal values with others, but rarely the exact set of personal values in priority order. For example, one person may place highest value on creativity, altruism, autonomy, adventure and learning. Another person may value achievement, challenge, physical activity, and prosperity. When we live our lives in alignment with our core values, we live an authentic, fulfilling life.

Our values are formed during childhood. Our genes, gender, upbringing, education, religion, ethnic group, income level, social roles, work environment, and political involvement are just a few factors influencing formation of our core values.[103] As we grow older, our peer groups exert additional influence. As we move into adulthood, we are consciously re-evaluating the values we formed in childhood and adolescence for their relevancy and priority to us. Our values are fairly stable, but can change over different life stages. For example, in our twenties, we may highly value achievement, status and money as we begin our careers. With the advent of children and family, we may place a higher value on work/life balance. Many of us have experienced a value shift in the later portion of our careers. We may seek more meaning and purpose in our lives today.

Most of the time we are on autopilot as we live our lives influenced by our highest priority values. We may not consciously notice as we drift from alignment with our core values. Our life choices may gradually be based more and more on work pressures and fulfilling the expectations of others. Being disconnected from our values can leave us with a vague and chronic sense of dissatisfaction. When we live in this disconnected state for years, our dissatisfaction undeniably bubbles to the surface. Many of the women interviewed spoke of a nagging dissatisfaction that fully surfaced when they reached their fifties and sixties. For some women, this disconnection from their core values served as a catalyst to actively plan their retirement.

Rediscovering or reconnecting with our core values is critical to creating a clear life purpose statement for our retirement. Depending on your preferences, there are two approaches included in this chapter. One approach is to begin with a blank canvas and work through a series of questions to derive core values. The second approach is to review a list of core values and select priorities values from this list **(Figure 6).** The latter approach does not prohibit adding additional values not appearing on the list.

CORE VALUES CHECKLIST©

From the list of core values below, identify your top 20. Once you have checked off your top 20, look at them again. Then highlight, by circling, your top ten. This list is not exhaustive, so feel free to add to it.

☐ Achievement	☐ Determination	☐ Harmony	☐ Purpose
☐ Accountability	☐ Directness	☐ Health	☐ Recognition
☐ Adventure	☐ Drive	☐ Helping others	☐ Religion
☐ Altruism	☐ Duty	☐ Honesty	☐ Resourcefulness
☐ Authenticity	☐ Economic security	☐ Humor	☐ Responsibility
☐ Authority	☐ Education	☐ Imagination	☐ Results
☐ Autonomy	☐ Efficiency	☐ Independence	☐ Risk taking
☐ Balance	☐ Empowerment	☐ Integrity	☐ Routine
☐ Beauty	☐ Environment	☐ Innovation	☐ Security
☐ Belonging	☐ Equality	☐ Intellectual status	☐ Serenity
☐ Boldness	☐ Excellence	☐ Justice	☐ Service
☐ Bravery	☐ Excitement	☐ Knowledge	☐ Sharing
☐ Calmness	☐ Expertise	☐ Leadership	☐ Skill
☐ Challenge	☐ Fairness	☐ Learning	☐ Solitude
☐ Change	☐ Faith	☐ Love	☐ Solving Problems
☐ Collaboration	☐ Fame	☐ Loyalty	☐ Solitude
☐ Commitment	☐ Family	☐ Meaning	☐ Status
☐ Community	☐ Fast Pace	☐ Money	☐ Success
☐ Compassion	☐ Flexibility	☐ Nature	☐ Teaching
☐ Competence	☐ Focus	☐ Openness	☐ Teamwork
☐ Competition	☐ Freedom	☐ Order	☐ Tradition
☐ Conformity	☐ Friendship	☐ Passion	☐ Travel
☐ Creativity	☐ Fun	☐ Peace	☐ Trust
☐ Curiosity	☐ Growth	☐ Power	☐ Variety
☐ Decisiveness	☐ Gratitude	☐ Privacy	☐ Wealth
☐ Dependability	☐ Happiness	☐ Productivity	☐ Winning
			☐ Wisdom

Dr. Rita Smith
See Change

Figure 6

Passion

When we are doing something we love, we find ourselves completely absorbed, with effortless concentration. Our minds are quiet, time is distorted, and we feel a heightened energy. Our whole being is engaged. We feel as though our heart is singing. We are connecting with our passion. For some people, their passion could be art, and for others it could be working with children. Again, our passions are individual to each of us. Our passions are intrinsically motivated. These are the activities that get us fired up! In his seminal work *Flow: The Psychology of Optimal Experience*, psychologist Mihaly Czikszentmihalyi presents his theory that people are happiest when they are in a state of flow. He describes this state as complete absorption with the activity at hand, with nothing else (food, time, ego, etc.) seeming to matter. [104] Some people refer to this as "being in the zone."

Surprisingly, many women interviewed had difficulty articulating their life passions. When asked, most paused, searching for the "answer." They just needed to reconnect with their authentic selves and engage in expansive thinking. Some of the questions we used to provoke a reconnection with their passions are listed below.

- If you had unlimited financial resources, what would you do?
- As a child, what did you love to do?

- When do you feel most alive?
- Describe a time when you were "in the zone." What you were doing?
- At the end of your life, what would you sorely regret not doing?
- What topic never seems bore you? What are you endlessly curious about?
- Do you ever feel you were born to do a particular thing? Describe this particular thing.

Working with these questions, spending time reflecting and experimenting in new areas helped these women move from a vague notion of their life passions to a place of energetic clarity. **Figure 7** provides a worksheet to reflect and record on what makes our heart sing.

WHAT MAKES YOUR HEART SING?©

The following questions will help you identify what makes your heart sing. Quickly brainstorm what comes up for you from your heart, not your head. Record your list below.

- What brings you joy?
- What gets you in a "flow" state, unaware of time and passionately focused?
- As a child, what did you love to do?
- When do you feel most alive?

Dr. Rita Smith
Visual Thinking Expert & Transitions Coach
See Change

Figure 7

Talent Shows

Scientists continue to investigate what comprises talent. Is it predominantly nature or environment? With recent findings on the brain's neuroplasticity for new learning, some point to the potential to develop talent. Other studies point to genetic determinacy of talent, citing physical attributes and generational talents. Consistently, scientists do agree that our DNA dictates a large portion of what we define as raw potential, aptitude, or talent. It is fair to conclude that each of us, to some extent, is hard-wired with natural talents.

Ironically, many people fail to recognize their talent. We assume something that is so natural and easy for us must be similarly natural and easy for others. This is more common in women, as we are more self-effacing then men. Or we believe a talent must be rarefied and difficult to execute. We point to Olympic athletes, opera singers, or master artists as those having talent. Most likely our talents were evident, to some extent, in childhood. Natural aptitude is enduring over time. One hint of an innate talent is when people describe us as "a natural" at a certain activity.

This is precisely why one highly effective way to uncover our natural talents is to invite others to describe what they see as our most dominant aptitudes. It is helpful to ask them to elaborate on the context surrounding their choice of a particular talent. Seek out multiple people from a variety of situations to obtain a robust, 360-degree view of our natural talents. Once we collect this data, review for common themes and compare against our own list of talents. Our combination of talents is unique to each of us. They are our own signature talents. **Figure 8** provides a place to record our signature talents, literally our unique gifts to share with the world. This exercise is organic. We may pursue a talent and find it is not as fulfilling as we originally projected, or we may experiment with a talent and find nirvana.

WHAT ARE YOUR GIFTS TO SHARE WITH THE WORLD?©

What talents and skills do you possess that you want to share with the world? Write the key words that describe your signature gifts in the arrows below.

Figure 8

Talents can be enhanced through development. From a talent development perspective, a person born with a natural talent for visual arts can increase the strength of their talent through study and practice. For example, Pablo Picasso, a pioneer in the Cubism style of art, was immersed in art education from age five until age sixteen. His art teacher father, aware of his son's love of drawing, immersed Pablo in intensive art education. At age sixteen, Pablo dropped out of art school, as he felt he was no longer learning. Retirement can provide us with the time to for education and practice of a dormant talent.

Talents can also be discovered when given the opportunity to reveal themselves. For example, a person with little opportunity to experiment with the visual arts, when given the opportunity, can discover a latent, natural talent. A well-known example of a late bloomer is Grandma Moses (Anna Mary Robertson Moses), the renowned folk artist. Although she showed an early interest in art and enjoyed creative household tasks like embroidery, her hardscrabble life left little opportunity for painting. As a young girl she worked as domestic, married and ran a farm, persevered through ten pregnancies and raised the five children who survived childbirth. At age seventy-eight, she dusted off an old paint set and began her painting in earnest. Retirement can also provide us with opportunity to experiment in areas that have been calling us for years.

One of my clients always enjoyed the creativity of baking, but between her career and raising a family, never had much time to devote to the pleasures of baking. After gathering observations about her natural talents from others, their mention of her baking aptitude validated her desire to explore this further. She enrolled in a pastry chef program at a local culinary school. Knowing this was diametrically opposed to her former career as an asset management executive, she viewed this program as an experiment. It turned out she loved and easily excelled in the program. She provides gourmet pastries for a local café and also volunteers, bringing her creations the local senior center.

Sir Ken Robinson, best-selling author of *Finding Your Element*, makes a critical observation that being in our "Element," that place of authentic fulfillment, is where our natural talents meet our passions.[105] When we both love something and have a natural aptitude for it, we easily launch into our "flow state." At the intersection of our values, passions, and talents is our life purpose. Our life purpose addresses our search for meaning and answers our introspective question, "Why am I here"?

Life Purpose: Why Am I Here?

Any major life transition triggers some level of introspection. We have seen this is most certainly the case with retirement transition. To reach the levels of senior leadership, we typically spent 20-30 years climbing the leadership mountain. We often logged in grueling 70-80 hour workweeks. Few of us had time to step off the work conveyer belt to comprehend the existential question, "Why am I here?" Besides, we were in the blush of youth, acquiring advanced degrees, ambitious, and perhaps embarking on creating a family. We thought we knew why we were here. Our own mortality was a nebulous concept. However, retirement changes all that.

Retirement signals the end of our primary career. At this time, we most likely have an empty nest when it comes to parenting duties. As we reach for our reading glasses and swallow our glucosamine, it is hard to deny we are entering the last decades of our lives. More time is behind us than ahead of us. We may have buried parents and have attended more funerals in the last ten years than the previous forty years. All of this creates fertile ground to plant the seeds of finding meaning and purpose---our legacy. At no other time in our lives does questioning the meaning of our lives become more intense.

If someone turned to us right now and asked, "What is your life purpose?" how would we respond? While the odds of someone asking us this question are small, the reality is that this question surrounds our lives and often goes unexamined. We tend to shirk from this question because it brings us face-to-face with our own mortality. Robert Leider, author of *The Power of Purpose Finding Meaning, Live Longer and Better*, states "to do that, we must make friends with death. Living purposefully means facing squarely the question of our own mortality." [106] A powerful exercise is to create our own eulogy. Imagine our friends and family stepping to the lectern to eulogize us. What was the impact of our lives? How do we wish to be remembered? And perhaps most profoundly, how does our current life reflect this essence of our impact and purpose? The worksheet in **Figure 9** helps us to craft this powerful exercise where the "rubber literally meets the road" to answer our question, "Did my life matter?" Despite the unease with exploring our own mortality, we innately know that our life purpose can live beyond us, bringing immortality to why we were here.

WRITING YOUR EULOGY

Imagine you are attending your own funeral. You watch as family and friends step to the podium to make their eulogy to you. They share the way you lived your life and your impact on the world around you. What do you want people to say about you? How do you want to be remembered. Take the time to jot down your thoughts below. It is powerful to see your thoughts in black and white!

To what degree does your current life reflect how you want people to remember you? How can you build yourself in to the person people described?

Figure 9

To succinctly articulate our life purpose, we must first be clear on what is important to us, what we love to do, and where our natural talents lie. Imagine a Venn diagram with values, passions, and talents intersecting into our life purpose. **Figures 9 and 10** help guide us in crafting our life purpose statement. Why is it important to actually write a life purpose statement? The process of crafting the statement engages us in reflection, prioritization, introspection, and ultimately expression of why our time on Earth matters. The output of this process is a single, inspiring statement that encompasses the answer to "Did my life matter?" The longevity and health benefits were presented in the opening of this chapter; however, on a day-to-day level, our life purpose statements provide us with motivation, clarity, decision criteria, and illuminates our way. When we share our life purpose statements with other, they become even more powerful and meaningful to us. No doubt we have a Last Will and Testament reflecting our wishes after we are gone. Our life purpose statement should have equal importance, as it reflects our wishes while we are here!

Much like our Last Will and Testament, our life purpose statement can be drafted and revised over time. It is typically not written in one setting, but rather builds on our work exploring our values, passions, and talents. A strong life purpose statement, similar to our former organizations' mission statements, defines who we are and why we do what we do. For example, Kellogg's purpose statement is

"Nourishing families so they can flourish and thrive."[107] In our life purpose statement, we specifically articulate our unique talents, directed to one or more of our passions, and describe the desired benefit. A retirement coaching client drafted the following life purpose statement: "My life purpose is to use my education and my love of learning, reading, and teaching so that illiteracy is eliminated in my community." Imagine attending this person's funeral service and hearing her described in these terms. Does this answer the question "Why was she here?" I believe so. This one statement alone gives her life meaning and a reason to awaken each morning and start her day filled with purpose. **Figures 10** provide templates to assist us in drafting our life purpose statement. When we have a draft with which we are satisfied, post it in a place to be seen each day and begin sharing it with others.

Creating our life purpose statement serves as the pivotal springboard from which we move to design a retirement life that powerfully reflects why we are here. In the next chapter, we will create a bold retirement life design.

RETIREMENT GPS:
CREATING YOUR LIFE PURPOSE STATEMENT©

My life purpose is to use

_____

(my unique talents/qualities)

to_____

(my passion)

_____

_____

So that _____

_____

_____

(meaningful legacy).

Figure 10

CHAPTER 9

"JUST MY IMAGINATION"

Temptations

So, What DO We Want?

Designing Women

Many of us led or participated in visioning meetings during the course of our professional careers. Design-thinking principles were most likely incorporated into these sessions to foster innovation. Brainstorming and ideation were the cornerstones. This time, the focus of our visioning is personal. To create the blueprint for our Retirement Lifestyle Plan, we will incorporate elements of design thinking and ideation tools. In the previous chapter, we gained clarity around our life purpose, or "why." In this chapter, we will leverage the self-discovery of our "why" to help create our "what"--the design for our reinvented self.

In the hallways of global design companies such as IDEO, the d. School of Stanford University, or companies like

Apple or Amazon, the process of design thinking is ubiquitous. Pick up an issue of *Fast Company Magazine* and inevitably an innovative company like Google, Netflix, Airbnb,
or Uber is featured for their design thinking. In a nutshell,
design thinking seeks solutions to a problem by first understanding the users, combining observation and research to
define where the users' problem exists, generating a range
of ideas, prototyping a selected range of ideas, testing with
users for feedback, and then implementation. The process
is human- versus product/solution-centered, iterative, non-
linear, emphasizing experimentation and collaboration.
However, design thinking is not only the purview of large
companies. The mindset and processes of design thinking
apply to our personal lives, as well. In *Designing Your Life:
How to Build a Well-Lived Joyful Life*, Stanford University design thinking experts Bill Burnett and Dave Evans encourage
us to use the same thinking that created the most amazing
technology, products, and spaces to design our lives. [108]

Ideation

As we explored our life purpose in Chapter Eight, in
effect, we began the process of understanding the user's
perspective on the problem. In this case the problem is "creating our retirement lifestyle." The user perspective is our
inner exploration of our values, passions, and ultimately our
life purpose. We are now ready to move into the divergent
thinking of brainstorming our dreams. "Designers learn to
have lots of wild ideas because they know the number one

enemy of creativity is judgment."[109] The goal here is to gen-erate multiple ideas without leaping to judgment. More ideas generate more choices and increase the innovative possibilities from which to choose. What dreams do we have inside us for our next decades?

When I Grow Up I Want to Be...

When we were children, the world had endless possi-bilities. We confidently declared our dreams of becoming a ballerina, rock star, president, scientist, artist, etc. We often pretended to be living these dreams, perhaps unabashedly playing our air guitars, pirouetting across our living rooms, or pretending to invent a magical solution to cure all diseases. Over time, perhaps a significant authority figure or societal pressures put a wet blanket on our dreams. A bias toward realism replaced our limitless imagination. As we grew older, our lives got in the way of these dreams. Daydreams still gave us glimpses of possibilities, but were fleeting.

As we craft our Retirement Lifestyle Plan, we have opportunity to uncover and reconnect with our buried dreams. We have opportunity to re-engage our authentic childhood sense of endless possibilities. In childhood, we spent our time playing. Many times, it is in our childhood play that clues for our future are found. Embarking on an archeological dig to uncover our childhood dreams is our launching point. Think back to our childhoods--what were our dreams? How did we reflect these dreams in our play? Make sure to create a list of these dreams.

One client shared that she recalls hours of playing that she was an adventurer discovering new lands. She remembers receiving a compass for her birthday. She reflected on this adventurer theme and realized she had buried her passion for discovery and nature. She wryly mentioned that she considered being a park ranger but was severely discouraged by her parents. They viewed this as a male career that would result in her "spinsterhood" and economic deprivation. She felt fear and powerlessness over their predictions. Her dreams of working in the wilderness, surrounded by the majesty of nature and sharing these wonders with visitors, were buried.

Take some time to create your list of childhood dreams. Reflect on these. What dreams should we add to our brainstorming list? Imagine that resources were not an issue-what activities, people, and experiences would we want in our lives? Now we can move from wide-open, divergent thinking to convergent thinking, culling our list to the dreams that align with our life purpose and energize us.

Catching Our Dreams

To ensure we capture our distilled list of amazing dreams, record these dreams on the worksheet in **Figure 11**. The graphic in **Figure 11** represents a Native American dream catcher, a Native American (linked to Ojibwe people) spiritual charm used historically by Indians to protect them during sleep. Native Americans believed the air was filled with dreams, both good and bad. They believed dreams prophesized future events, offered spiritual guidance, and provided spiritual symbolism that results in a child's name or a lifetime personal totem. "The traditional dream catcher was intended to protect the sleeping individual from negative dreams, while letting positive dreams through. The positive dreams would slip through the hole in the center of the dream catcher, and glide down the feathers to the sleeping person below. The negative dreams would get caught up in the web, and expire when the first rays of the sun struck them."[110]

I CAN SEE CLEARLY NOW: DREAM CATCHER©

Catching Your Retirement Dreams: Originating from the Ojibwa (Chippewa) Nation, dream catcher's were believed to alter a person's dreams by protecting the sleeper from negative dreams by catching these bad dreams inside its web. Good dreams filter through the center hole and descend down the feathers to the dreamer. The slightest movement of the feathers would indicate the passage of another beautiful dream. Bad dreams however were trapped in the web and would be burned off by the morning sun.

What retirement dreams do you want to "catch"? Record them in the arrows below.

Figure 11

Dream catchers typically consist of wooden hoops filled with netting or web. The hoop represents the circle of life. Hanging from the hoop are feathers and beads. The feathers help the good dreams glide into the dreamer's mind. The beads represent the good dreams trapped during the night. Collecting our dreams on our own dream catcher worksheet taps into an ancient spiritual belief in the power of our dreams.

Prototying

In design thinking, prototyping is about testing ideas and obtaining feedback. In some cases, it involves creating a low-fi version of a product or simulating an experience. Prototyping reduces uncertainty and provides feedback before the project moves into costly production and implementation. As we create our Retirement Lifestyle Plan, it makes sense to experiment with our dreams to obtain feedback. For example, the client who gave up her childhood dreams of being a park ranger identified that her dream of spending time in nature and sharing its beauty with others was still valid. She conducted research and concluded that becoming a park ranger would not make sense for her at this point. However, she explored other possibilities. A beautiful, mountainous state park was only 45 minutes from her home. Her "prototyping" included experimenting with a role there. First, she arranged to meet with the park's executive director and program director to explore potential roles. Their volunteer program included guided nature tours and talks. Before committing to volunteering, she requested to shadow other volunteers. She even assisted with a few nature tours. This experimentation provided her with direct feedback to aid her decision of implementing her dream as a volunteer at the state park.

Spending time researching, interviewing, shadowing, and experiencing (simulated or real time) our dreams is one of the most important steps in the design thinking process. As we move to more certainty about our dream lifestyle, we can use our "right brain" visual creativity to create a powerful picture of our exciting next phase.

Dream Boards

A Dream Board or Vision Board is a visual representation of all the things that we want to do, be, and have in our lives. It is an inspirational collage comprised of visuals or pictures with few key words that provides a tangible representation of our future. In recent years, Dream Boards were made popular by the book *The Secret,* which discusses the Law of Attraction and the role of Dream Boards in harnessing our energy to realize our goals.[111] Law of Attraction advocates believe "what we think about will come about."

From a neuroscience perspective, Dream Boards focus on our feelings and connections to images, allowing us access to our subconscious mind. The process of creating a Dream Board is typically motivating, leaving us feeling happily inspired. These emotions trigger release of dopamine, the positive-feeling neurotransmitter. [112] This neurotransmitter plays a strong role in motivation and energizes us to take inspired action toward our goals. Every time we look at our Dream Boards, we create new neural pathways resulting in new ways to look at our goals and new actions to achieve them. Finally, in frequently viewing our Dream Board, we imprint the dream images on our brains. This is called reticular activation, where we unconsciously become more aware of connections and opportunities that help us achieve the goals of our Dream Board. [113] Even when we don't realize we are thinking about these goals, our brain knows that they're important and makes note of anything that might relate to them.

Whether we ascribe to the power of the universe to manifest our dreams through the Law of Attraction or are more science-based, Dream Boards have value, in both the process of creating them and the content of the finished product.

Creating Our Dream Boards

Creativity has limitless possibilities. So do our Dream Boards. Over the years, my clients have created everything from the classic poster board collage to 3-D objects, cork board collages, giant wall collages, framed collages, and paintings. A few cleverly photographed their Dream Board and used this as their computer and smartphone wallpaper to further the visual reminders. **Figure 12** depicts an example of a Dream Board.

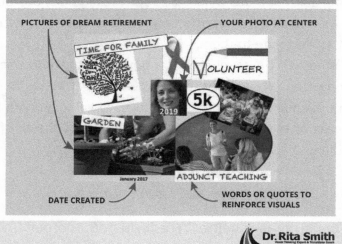

I CAN SEE CLEARLY NOW: CREATING YOUR VISION BOARD©

WHAT IS A VISION BOARD? A vision board is a goal-setting tool using images and words to clarify your goals, focus your actions, and generate motivation. The process of creating your vision board helps distill what is most important to you and aligned with your values. The very process of selecting pictures engages both reflection and emotion. Science tells us humans are wired to process information visually. Studies of brain neuroplasticity (brain's ability to change) also supports the power of visuals in stimulating neuron activity. From a different perspective, vision boards support the key Law of Attraction tenet, "what you think about, comes about". Vision boards help attract, or manifest, what you want in your life. The bottom line is that focusing and envisioning your goals is a highly effective tool to achieve your retirement vision. Remember you are focusing on the WHAT here, not the HOW.

VISION BOARD EXAMPLE: The vision board pictured below was completed using on-line images. (See Vision Board resource page) Use your creativity. There is no precise formula to create a vision board—there are no rules! Once you have your supplies gathered (See Vision Board checklist page), review your Life Purpose and Values Checklist. Look for images that depict your WHY which will lead you to your WHAT.

Figure 12

Dream Board collages focus primarily on pictures, with a few key, powerful words. The process of paging through old magazines, photos, and travel guides and selecting pictures taps into your inspiration. Typical life planning engages left-brain methods such as logical, sequential, and analytical thinking. Approaching the creation of our Dream Boards from the right brain leverages creative, random, intuitive, and holistic thinking. There are times when words simply are inadequate to convey a desire or feeling.

The following instructions are merely suggestions. These are not meant to be directive or prescriptive. Fencing in our creativity is not the goal; rather, the goal is set it free! Anchored to and informed by our life purpose statements and dream catcher dreams, place an image or powerful word in the center of the collage. This is our theme or focal point. For example: "Meaning," "My Time," "Living Purposefully," "Connecting with Nature," "Giving Back," "Soul Art," "Me 2.0," etc. The images we select should elaborate on this theme. We may want to elaborate on our images with a powerful key word or brief phrase. Many people find these key words in the magazines and resources they used for selecting inspirational images. An example of adding a key word to a selected image is a client who wanted to become a "14er," hiking Colorado mountain peaks 14,000 feet and above. She placed a beautiful image of a Colorado mountain on her collage and added the NIKE phrase "Just Do It" to the image.

Online options to create Dream Boards are available, as well. Clip art can augment our other images. In addition, there are websites that offer tools to create an online Dream Board. A Google search yields many such options. Some clients have not only printed their online Dream Board but also enlarged it into a poster.

Every Dream Board is unique. The Dream Board product is important, but the process of creation connects us to our deepest inspiration. Expect a dopamine release! The key to our Dream Boards is to make them visible to be seen every day. The daily visual reinforcement imprints the images of our retirement dreams upon on our brain. A couple months after creating her Dream Board, a client shared she did not continue to feel inspired by her Dream Board. After more discussion, it turns out she had placed her Dream Board in a closet, removing the power of daily, visual reinforcement. When she moved her Dream Board over her desk, she reported feeling the connection once again.

Included in the "Heard It Through the Grapevine" Appendix section of this book is a list of Dream Board resources. These resources provide everything from detailed supply lists and examples to reinforcement strategies to make our Dream Boards even more powerful.

What to Do With All That Time?

No more alarm clocks. No more meetings. No more unrealistic deadlines. No more office politics. For the first time in our lives since perhaps our pre-kindergarten years, we will have the time to do whatever we chose. Upon retirement, each of us is gifted with minimally an additional seven hours per day of leisure. Leisure is defined here as having work-free time that we can choose how we spend it. We may have put off a cruise, an artistic endeavor, spending time with grandchildren, and/or other "bucket list" activities. We retire and enthusiastically jump into these activities.

Months down the road, we realize these activities do not fill our new seven hours of leisure per day. We have time on our hands. We have a nagging feeling we are squandering our precious commodity of retirement time. We are more acutely aware of the dichotomy of having so much time in retirement but also so little time left, as retirement comes in the last stage of our life. A 2016 research study conducted by Merrill Lynch and Age Wave, the later a research organization on population aging, found that very few of us actually plan for our new leisure time. When age 50+ retirees were asked how much planning they had done for the next five year of leisure, 77% responded hardly any, 19% some, an only 4% stated a lot. [114] It is ironic that we were highly effective at planning during our careers. We were highly effective at our retirement financial planning. However, planning for our leisure is truly uncharted territory. It is no surprise that traditional retirees with little or no lifestyle planning spend approximately 50% of their free time watching television.[115]

Our history with leisure is typically spotted. For 30-40 years of our professional careers, our leisure was limited to evenings, weekends, and vacations. Well, sort of vacations. The aforementioned Merrill Lynch and Age Wave research study described our workaholic US culture as the "no-vacation nation."[116] Compared to other industrialized nations, we average 11 paid days of vacation versus the 22-30 days of paid vacation time enjoyed by countries like Germany, Brazil, and the United Kingdom. [117] Here is another "fun fact" on our workaholic culture--the US government does not mandate that employers provide any paid vacation or holidays to workers unlike nearly all the other industrialized nations. [118] Not all of this workaholism is the fault of our government. Only 41% of employed American workers who do receive paid time off use all of this vacation time. [119] Then when we do take vacations, a high percentage of us are checking our emails and doing other work-related activities. Does this sound all too familiar?

On the surface, planning for our leisure sounds like an oxymoron. However, as we have seen with the above statistics, we simply do not have much experience with leisure, let alone planning for it. Research studies repeatedly find the better management of leisure time correlated with a happier and more fulfilling retirement. [120] Retirees who manage free time well enjoy a higher quality of life. Those retirees who have no plan for their free time typically experience boredom and a sedentary lifestyle. From this emotional and physical place, it is far too easy for our psychic dominos to begin to fall. We begin to question our value. We deeply question our decision to retire. We begin frenetic activity unconnected to our life purpose. We did not sacrifice and work for decades to grab the brass ring of retirement and find it tarnished.

Viewing our retirement time as a precious resource is key. During our careers, we successfully managed our organization's resources. Successful management was predicated upon solid planning practices. We are given an unprecedented longevity bonus and have the financial means to make this period of time the capstone of our life's fulfillment. How will we allocate our time?

I'll Take a Slice

Creating a pictorial representation of our time is extremely useful to our planning process. When we retired, we probably assumed the rows and columns of spreadsheet software were left behind. Well, for the most part, yes. However, dusting off our spreadsheet software, a pie chart is the perfect tool with which to create a picture of how we will spend our time. **Figure 13** provides a pie chart worksheet tool.

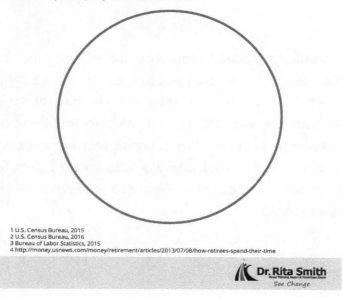

HOW WILL YOU SPEND YOUR NEW FREE TIME?©

2,000 Hours of Free Time: Retirees suddenly find themselves with approximately 2,000 annual hours of free time previously devoted to work. This equates to 7.5 new leisure hours daily [1]. Collectively, over the next two decades, 2.5 trillion leisure hours[2] will be created by retiring Baby Boomers. After years of structured schedules, leisure time to do with as you wish sounds absolutely wonderful, doesn't it? In practicality, however studies show that over 95%[3] of retirees have no plan for how to maximize this new free time. Studies show traditional retirees spend their time doing the following: approximately 50% of their free time watching television, 30% dedicated to household activities (home improvements, cooking, laundry), 10% eating, and the remaining 10% reading, shopping and socializing.[4] Is this truly the retirement life plan suited to Baby Boomers? How will YOU spend your free time?

In the "pie chart" below, representing 100% of your new, annual leisure time of 2,000 hours, indicate how you will spend your retirement leisure time.

1 U.S. Census Bureau, 2015
2 U.S. Census Bureau, 2016
3 Bureau of Labor Statistics, 2015
4 http://money.usnews.com/money/retirement/articles/2013/07/08/how-retirees-spend-their-time

Dr. Rita Smith
See Change

Figure 13

This is a directional exercise; thus, we need to suspend our desire for precision. Imagine it is New Year's Eve and we are reflecting back on how we used our time in the past year. Assume our past year was fulfilling and meaningful. Create an initial list of how time (percentages) was allocated resulting in this successful retirement year. Think of categories such as family, health/fitness, socializing, volunteering, paid employment, personal development (classes/reading/ workshops), spirituality, hobbies, travel, relaxation, and maintaining our home tasks. Feel free to add other categories, as well.

Once we have a comparatively stable list of activities and their associated percentages of time, we can depict this on our pie chart. Our pie chart provides us a visual snapshot of our major time allocations during an average year of our retirement. Does our pie align with our life purpose? Are our personal values clearly evident in our choices? Does our pie chart move us toward our dreams? If our response to any of these questions is uncertainty or a clear no, we need to continue to work this exercise. If our response to these questions is yes, then we are ready to visibly post our pie chart as a guide for how we choose to spend our time.

In this chapter, we borrowed from the applicable best practices of design thinking. After all, the focus of this stage in the Reinventing Boomer Retirement Roadmap is creation of blueprint design for our retirement lifestyle. We employed brainstorming and user (ourselves!) feedback in our ideating. We reconnected with childhood dreams and manifested new ones. These dreams were "caught" in our dream catchers. We may have prototyped a few of our dreams to gather additional feedback on our design. We moved to make our dreams more tangible through the power of visual images. Our Dream Boards and time pie charts move us one step closer to implementing our lifestyle plan.

Do we have "the right stuff" to achieve our retirement lifestyle dreams? What internal and external resources need to be in place to ensure success? The next chapter provides exercises to answer these questions and move even closer to implementation.

CHAPTER 10

"TICKET TO RIDE"

Beatles

Do We Have the Right Stuff?

Reaching In and Reaching Out

Fresh out of college, we embarked on our first job hunt. We had a target role in mind. We assessed our strengths, skills, and weaknesses against what the role required. We worked to close relevant, critical gaps. We did our research and identified job opportunities that best aligned with our strengths. We thought through potential threats such as competition and the organization's stability. As we journey into our retirement lifestyle, we need to replicate this same type of process. Our "ticket to ride" requires both a candid assessment process and asking for assistance.

Personal SWOT Analysis

Most of us utilized the structured analysis and planning tool, the "SWOT" Analysis, in the course of our careers.

"SWOT" stands for strengths, weaknesses, opportunities, and threats. Many organizations use this tool as part of their strategic planning. Although the origin of the SWOT tool is debated, we do know that it first appeared in the 1950s and 1960s at Stanford and Harvard Universities. Using a SWOT tool provides an internal and external assessment of the current state. It identifies strengths to leverage, weaknesses to mitigate, uncovers opportunities to pursue, and threats to consider. Few of us, however, have ever applied this tool to our own lives.

From an internal perspective, that which we have direct influence to impact or change, are our strengths and weaknesses. **Figures 14** provides resources with which we can complete our own personal SWOT analysis. Our strengths are our skills, competencies, personality traits, knowledge, and experiences at which we excel. To help trigger creating our list of strengths, ask: "What are my life's peak accomplishments?" Reflecting on these accomplishments will reveal areas of strength. What do others see as our strengths? What qualities do others admire in us? We may have initial success in readily identifying a list of our strengths. In all likelihood, though, there are less-obvious strengths that require a third party to identify. We can include our trusted inner circle for candid and honest feedback.

Do You Have the Right Stuff ?: Conducting a Personal S.W.O.T.©

Conducting a Personal S.W.O.T.: Perhaps you are already familiar with the S.W.O.T. This process is commonly used in organizations to assess themselves as they create and plan to execute on their strategies. S.W.O.T. stands for S= Strengths (internal), W=Weaknesses (internal), O= Opportunities (external) and T = Threats (external).

Used on a personal level, this process captures information about your favorable strengths and what favorable external opportunities and resources are readily available to you. Likewise, your Personal S.W.O.T. assesses areas of weakness such as gaps in required skills or knowledge, time constraints, fears and other internal obstacles and gaps that are barriers in executing your retirement life plan. Finally, it assesses external threats and obstacles, such as limited demand for your area of interest, lack of volunteer roles, potential competition, etc.

Conduct an honest and fearless assessment. Share your Personal S.W.O.T. with people who are candidly able to assess your strengths and weaknesses. Share your assessment with people who have insight into the external opportunities and threats to your retirement life plan . Finally, use your assessment data to inform provide your action plan. Given your S.W.O.T. assessment, what gaps do you need to close?, what threats do you need to mitigate?, what opportunities can you leverage?, what strengths can you leverage and build upon?

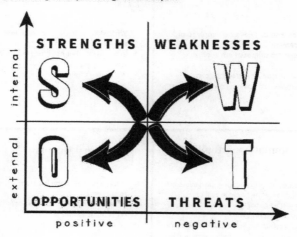

Figure 14

Do You Have the Right Stuff ?: Conducting a Personal S.W.O.T.©

Conducting a Personal S.W.O.T. : To maximize the outcome of this exercise, ensure you have quiet reflection time to complete your Personal S.W.O.T.   The questions below are intended to jumpstart your thinking and are certainly not an exhaustive list of inquiries.

Clients report it is helpful to first brainstorm their assessment using sticky notes. This allowed them to combine and/or edit before their final personal assessment was complete.

 Internal Strengths

- What skills do I have that apply to my retirement vision?
- People typically say I am good at _____?
- What personality strengths can I leverage to achieve my retirement life plan?

 Internal Weaknesses

- What skills or knowledge do I need to attain?
- In the past, what has hindered me from achieving goals?
- What am I afraid of?

 External Opportunities

- What education and/or experiences are available for me to close skill or knowledge gaps?
- Who can support me?
- What resources can I tap into to ensure my retirement vision becomes a reality?

 External Threats

- What external obstacles are in my way to success?
- What macro trends could affect my retirement vision?
- What competition exists?

Figure 14

Do You Have the Right Stuff ?: Personal S.W.O.T.©

S Internal Strengths	**W** Internal Weaknesses
O External Opportunities	**T** External Threats

Figure 14

EMPTY NEST, EMPTY DESK, WHAT'S NEXT?

Naturally, reflecting on our weaknesses holds limited appeal. However, as human beings, we do have weaknesses. Self-awareness and owning these weaknesses will make our Retirement Lifestyle Plan that much stronger. Reflect on what we find more difficult to accomplish than other people. In what areas are we less confident? For example, public speaking is often an area of discomfort for many. Think back to our years of performance reviews. Are there personality traits, competencies, or skill gaps that were repeatedly identified? Again, engaging our trusted inner circle will help us to identify our weaknesses. Once we complete our personal SWOT analysis, we will assess our list of weaknesses against the other elements of our completed SWOT. We may opt to develop a relevant weakness, convert it into strength, neutralize it, or even decide it requires no attention, as it is irrelevant to our lifestyle plan.

From an external perspective, the SWOT elements are opportunities and threats. Opportunities include areas such as trends, resources, education, work and volunteer roles, etc. Our strengths usually point us to potential opportunities. For example, strengths in leadership, public speaking, relationship building, and visual arts could point to opportunities either paid or volunteer in community outreach for a museum. Each of us has a unique combination of signature strengths that correspond to individualized opportunities.

Threats are external dangers or barriers to our lifestyle plans. These can include a range of potential obstacles out of our control. Things such as economic issues, competition, and changing trends are just a few such obstacles. Although we cannot control external threats, we can factor their potentiality into our plans by including options and flexibility.

Assembling A Dream Team

A tremendous resource for our determining if we have the "right stuff" is the collective wisdom of our own personal Board of Directors. The term Board of Directors probably evokes an image of a group of people, in business suits, seated around a large conference table. We may have presented to this type of governing board during our professional careers, as their responsibilities include setting policy, objectives, and overall direction for an organization. In addition, they have fiduciary oversight for the organization's shareholders or key stakeholders. When we review an organization's Board of Directors roster, we typically see accomplished people with diverse backgrounds. These are the type of people we want for our personal Board of Directors, or "Dream Team."

Our personal Board of Directors should serve as a wise, honest, and confidential sounding board. They should have strong opinions and viewpoints balanced with a non-judgmental approach. Within the group we need people with strengths to challenge, seek clarification, and connect us with resources and opportunities. Management educator and best-selling author Jim Collins states that "the best board members dispense wisdom like Socrates—by asking questions, drawing analogies, and making dispassionate observations."[121]

Target 4-6 people. Naturally, we need to be clear about our expectations of these people prior to our contacting them. What is the purpose of our Board? What is the term of service? How often will we meet? Will this be in-person, virtually, or both? Meeting frequency is typically monthly in the early part of our planning and then moves to a quarterly basis. Clarify that this is a pro bono request. Prepare to be surprised by the number of "yes" responses. It is a paradox that highly accomplished and in-demand potential personal Board members are typically very willing to support the development of others. They embody the concept of "paying it forward." Perhaps they were the recipients of generous mentors contributing to their success. **Figure 15** is a planning worksheet to assist in assembling our personal Board of Directors.

Do You Have the Right Stuff ?: Your Personal Board of Directors ©

Selecting your "Personal Board of Director's " or "Dream Team": First, look beyond your family and close friends who are naturally emotionally invested in you. You want people who will not be biased by their emotional connection with you. Seek people with diverse backgrounds to maximize a variety of perspectives. Be very clear what strengths each person brings to the group and how you plan to leverage these strengths

Name:_____

Key Strength(s):
_____
_____
____

Name:_____

Key Strength(s):
_____
_____
____

Dream Team

Name:_____

Key Strength(s):
_____
_____
____

Name:_____

Key Strength(s):
_____
_____
____

Name:_____

Key Strength(s):
_____
_____
____

Name:_____

Key Strength(s):
_____
_____
____

Figure 15

A client seeking to start a small, all-natural online pet supply store created her personal Board of Directors comprised of six people. As her pre-retirement background was finance, she sought out expertise in online retailing, online marketing, logistics, small business launches, accounting, and a retired veterinarian. The group initially met in-person for their first meeting. All of the personal Board members lived within a short train or driving distance. For this first meeting, she distributed a pre-meeting draft of her business plan. Her objectives for the first meeting, beyond introductions and confirmation of the Board's purpose, was to review her vision, mission, and to review her Business Model Canvas. The latter is a wonderful, one-page visual tool used to identify and then align business activities. It contains elements such as target customers, value proposition, key resources, channels, revenue structure, etc. It is most effectively used as a prelude to a more detailed business plan or to examine an existing business model. (It was first introduced by Alexander Osterwalder in 2008 and is available as a free download from a number of sources. *The Business Model Canvas handbook, Business Model Generation: A Handbook for Visionaries, Game Changers, and Challengers*, by Osterwalder and Pigneur (2010) is available through major booksellers.)

Subsequent meetings reviewed next iterations and finally her detailed business plan. In addition, to business start-up consulting, her personal Board provided her with additional resources and connections to enhance her business plan. Once her online business launched, she conducted a virtual meeting twice a year. She also distributed quarterly and annual progress reports. After the second year in business, she downshifted to an annual meeting and an annual report. The following year, she disbanded her personal Board. It was a pleasure to watch this client leverage her personal Board, giving her the wise counsel, connections, and confidence to move forward with her entrepreneurial venture.

Hook-Ups

Hook-up may have a different connotation for younger generations today, but here it refers to networking. It is about connecting with others to build advantageous relationships. Ultimately, these relationships can provide us with resources to further our retirement lifestyle dreams. Meeting a variety of people with whom to develop relationships can yield specific opportunities, knowledge, further people connections, and a host of other resources. However, we may not be as proficient as we would like.

Many professional Boomer women focused so exclusively on their careers that little time was left to engage in networking. Many clients reported retiring and then realizing they only have a small network related to their former careers. As we know, the shelf life of these work-related networks diminishes rather quickly once current employees and vendors view us as irrelevant. Clients were truly at a loss as to where to begin, and slightly panicked, knowing that it takes time to form solid networking relationships.

Their advice is to begin investing in non-work networks prior to retirement, if at all possible. A secondary challenge for women is our struggles with self-promotion. Crafting a solid "elevator speech" about our life purpose and key retirement dreams will help us engage with new people in networking scenarios.

As we reached our middle age years, we witnessed the explosion of social networking. Sites such as Facebook, Twitter, Meetup, Google+, and Tumblr are now part of our daily lexicon. These are all potential avenues for us to post articles, blog, attend virtual meetings, and connect with others who can help us move closer to our dream retirement. Often overlooked when we retire, we need to keep our online profiles updated and reflecting our life purpose and the retirement dreams we are pursuing. Upon connecting with us, people will check out our social media presence. In other words, our powerfully crafted LinkedIn profiles do not end the day we retire, but rather require reinvention to reflect our retirement journey. Online social networking is definitely powerful; however, it should be just one channel in our overall networking portfolio. There are knowledge networks, groups that meet to specifically build professional relationships, and a host of Boomer retirement groups. Local business journals are a good resource in listing networking meetings. Lists of national and local Boomer retirement groups, such as Encore.org (focusing on engaging the talents of midlife and older men and women), are listed in the Appendix.

Dr. Ivan Misner, a networking guru and Founder and Chairman of Business Network International advises, "Be visible. Networking is a contact sport! You have to get out and connect with people." [122] We need a diverse network to maximize meeting people who can connect us with people we would never have met otherwise. These people then connect us with additional people, and so on, and so on. As we embark on our networking, experts recommend we create a game plan of who or what type of people with whom to connect. **Figure 16** provides a worksheet to identify key, relevant, and current network contacts as well as add names of people or organizations to explore. Networking experts further recommend keeping records so that we can track our efforts to connect with these contacts. That's right--dust off the spreadsheet software again. Keeping track of contact date, method of contact, and specific notes about our contacts can foster stronger relationships. One client employs a spreadsheet and devotes a minimum of one hour per day to developing her post-retirement network. She adeptly and systematically sends out pertinent articles, recognizes birthdays, and seeks out ways to help her contacts.

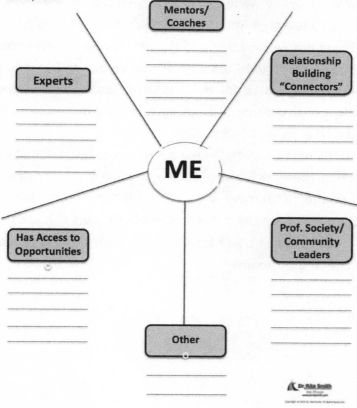

Do You Have the Right Stuff ?: Mapping My Power Network©

Mapping My Power Network: Networks are relationships that are critical to your ability to learn new skills, access desired opportunities, and advance toward your goal. Being intentional about whom you want in your Power Network is key. In the spaces below, list the names of people you would like to have in your retirement life plan network. Identify network areas requiring further development.

Mentors/ Coaches

Experts

Relationship Building "Connectors"

ME

Has Access to Opportunities

Prof. Society/ Community Leaders

Other

Figure 16

From Right Stuff to Making It Happen

Our SWOT analysis, identification of our potential personal Board of Directors, and our networking game plan yields rich areas for development and related activities. Before moving to the next chapter, "Making It Happen," it is helpful if we capture our key strategies to close gaps we uncovered. While we identified many strengths and opportunities to leverage in our SWOT analysis, the key gaps recorded in our weaknesses and threats do require attention. We may have a good amount of homework and planning to identify and plan for our personal Board of Directors. Finally, our assessment of our current network most likely identified gaps we need to close.

In the next chapter, "Making It Happen," we will pull together all the work we have done in the first four steps of our Reinventing Retirement Roadmap. This last step, Making It Happen, is where the proverbial rubber meets the road as we create a realistic and actionable plan for the retirement lifestyle of our dreams.

"DREAMWEAVER"

Gary Wright

Creating a Powerful Action Plan

Turning Our Dreams Into Plans

Some of us may remember our parents bringing us outside to spot the Soviet satellite Sputnik soar across the night sky. The technical achievement by our Cold War enemies, symbolized by this beach-ball-sized satellite, ignited fear in our parents' minds. Minimally, Boomers recall growing up during the "Space Race." On July 21, 1969, many of us watched the grainy black and white images of the historic *Apollo 11* moon landing. We incredulously watched Neil Armstrong and Buzz Aldrin skip across the lunar surface *Apollo 11* effectively ended the Space Race and fulfilled a national goal proposed in 1961 by US President John F. Kennedy: "Before this decade is out, of landing a man on the Moon and returning him safely to the Earth."[123]

President John F. Kennedy's goal to land man on the moon and return him safely was the vision--the dream. Without a powerful action plan, President Kennedy's inspirational motivational vision would have been just that a vision, not a reality.

NASA *Apollo 11* leaders were tasked with implementation. They shared, "As planning for *Apollo* began, we identified more than 10,000 separate tasks that had to be accomplished to put a man on the Moon. Each task had its particular objectives, its manpower needs, its time schedule, and its complex interrelationship with many other tasks. Which had to be done first? Which could be done concurrently? What were the critical sequences? Vital questions such as these had to be answered in building the network of tasks leading to a lunar landing."[124]

Similarly, we desire for our retirement dreams to move into a reality for us. And, similarly, we need to create a powerful plan for action. Our planning will comprise two levels: the macro, big steps level and a more tactical level of detailed actions to support the big steps. During the course of our professional careers, we used planning tools to execute strategy and to implement projects. We know, firsthand, that action plans help us prioritize, focus, instill accountability, enhance motivation, and monitor progress. At this critical juncture of executing on our dream retirement lifestyle, an action plan is imperative.

After working the Reinventing Retirement Roadmap

exercises, we are clear about our values, life purpose, dreams, strengths and areas for development, opportunities, and threats and needed resources. From this, a few big action steps should emerge. See **Figure 17**. For example, a client who is a former Human Resources EVP was clear that her life purpose was to preserve and share her family's history for future generations and to help minority executives successfully transition to roles of senior leadership. These goals became her "What next?" four-year plan. Specifically, her goals were twofold: 1) creating an in-depth book on her family history to share with future generations, and 2) launching an executive coaching practice targeting minority leaders. These two goals became her overriding action steps. From these, she identified specific actions that would advance and support her success in achieving these goals.

Making It Happen: Five Key Action Steps©

Choosing Your Five Key Action Steps: Review your Closing Gaps © worksheet. From your list of gaps and strategies to close these gaps, what are your top five Big Actions critical to making your Re-Invented Retirement happen? In the spaces below, list the action and target completion date. Identify who will serve as your accountability partner. From this list you may want to create a more detailed project plan. Please see the Sample Action Plan Timeline on the next page.

MY ACCOUNTABILITY PARTNER:_____

My Re-Invented Retirement

Big Action # 5:
Target Date:

Big Action # 4:
Target Date:

Big Action #3:
Target Date:

Big Action #2:
Target Date:

Big Action #1:
Target Date:

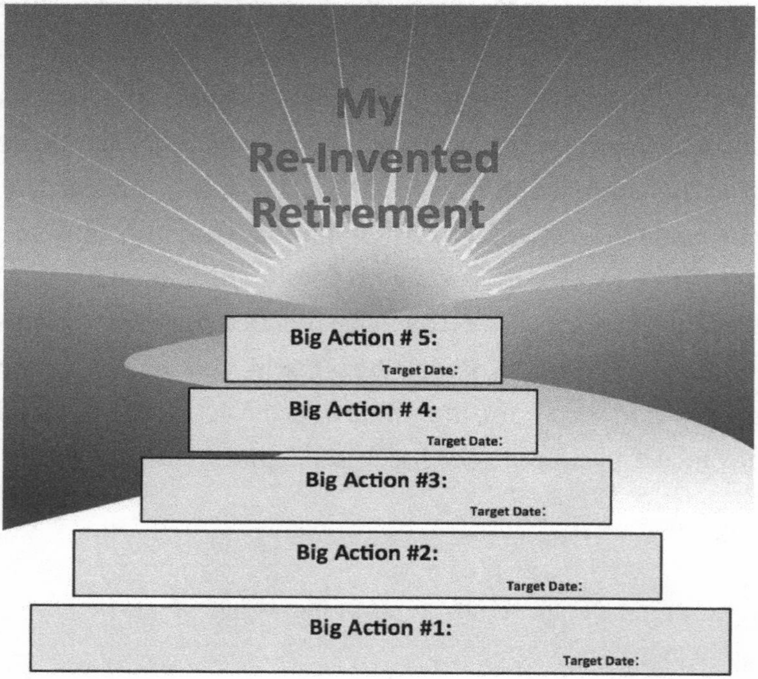

Figure 17

Her personal SWOT analysis helped her identify opportunities, strengths, gaps, and potential threats. The data from this exercise fed into her more tactical action plan. She divided her tactical plan into increments of one year, totaling three years. Beginning with the end goal in mind, she worked her way back to identify sequential actions. For example, to create a book on her family history, she recognized she needed education in the field of genealogy. Year One, she sought to take online courses working toward a certification in genealogy. This required her to first research educational resources, enroll, and then begin her studies. Connecting with others who succeed in this field was another activity in Year One. Finally, she committed to organizing her current family history and photos.

For Year Two, she slated completing her genealogy certification, interviewing family to gather primary research and stories, volunteering with her city's genealogy society, and researching her family history back to the 1500s.

Year Three actions included traveling key family history locations for further on-site research, working with a genealogy expert coach, and creating a detailed outline for her book.

Year Four focused upon writing her family history book, inclusive of editing assistance, and self-publishing. This client similarly addressed her second goal of executive coaching for minority leaders with sequential action steps.

Keeping Us On Track: An Accountability Partner

Keeping our Big Action Steps and Tactical Action Steps visible is important to reinforcing our dreams and maintaining motivation. As we accomplish key actions, this gives us opportunity to visibly record this milestone and celebrate. Perhaps most important is obtaining an accountability partner. Simon Sinek, author of the best-selling book *Start with*

Why, observes that human beings are social animals and will be more likely to achieve a goal when we are responsible to others. [125] We can find accountability partners in working with a coach, by joining or establishing a mastermind accountability group, and/or working with a designated accountability partner whom we trust to hold us to our very highest standard of achievement. Studies abound underscoring the importance of accountability strategies and success in achieving goals. Stanford University researchers conducted a study in 2007, where two groups of people were given an exercise program. Half of the group received weekly "accountability" phone calls every two weeks to check in on their progress, and the other half did not. The Stanford research showed that the group receiving "accountability" calls increased their amount of exercise by an average of 78%. [126] Virginia Polytechnic University conducted a similar study with weekly accountability phone calls over a period of 24 weeks. Those who received the weekly accountability calls were 1600% more likely to stick to their exercise program than those who did not.[127]

Working the Room; Working Our Plan

We are well on our way to making our dreams for a reinvented retirement lifestyle a reality. We are creating our new retirement identity. We did the heavy lifting of introspection, assessment, and planning. Typically, a big part of our plans will involve networking and asking others for assistance. Throughout our careers, we probably carried business cards identifying our professional title and contact information. This 2 X 3 card stock summarized our professional identity and provided practical information on how to reach us. Exchanging tangible business cards. The generations behind us may challenge the lack of eco-consciousness of our using business cards. Most likely they will accept our business card, take a smartphone picture to digitalize it, and then toss it into the nearest trashcan. However, a number of people clearly see the value of business cards. This is evident with Vistaprint's continuing success providing printing services for business cards and other marketing materials. Vistaprint, an e-commerce digital marketing services company, continues its double-digit growth with 2016 annual revenues of $1.4 billion, with over 30% of this revenue coming from the printing of business cards. [128] They are known for highly affordable, high-quality business cards. These can be created from scratch or via a user-friendly template. While some may view the exchange of business cards a waning tradition, the growth of small and microbusinesses' demand for business cards continues. Also, other global cultures such as Asian cultures view their business cards as an extension of themselves. These cultures have elaborate rituals surrounding the exchange of business cards.

Yes, the practice of exchanging business cards has its roots in historic tradition. In the 19th century, the idea of a personal "business" card came into practice. Wealthier society would drop off their "calling cards." These cards contained their name and perhaps a note, as a means to make an introduction or to further an acquaintance. In the 1890s, growing industrialization extended the "calling card" concept to businesses. While LinkedIn provides an important professional profile, business cards still have a place in our networking.

As we begin working our plan, we will no doubt be "working the room," or networking. Investing in a personal "business" card reinforces and concretely announces our evolving new identity. From a practical standpoint, it provides others with our logistics information. **Figure 18** provides a worksheet to assist in designing our personal "business" cards, signifying that we have crossed over to reinventing retirement selves.

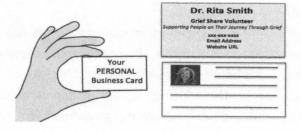

I Can See Clearly Now: Your PERSONAL " Business" Card©

Key things to consider when creating your PERSONAL "Business" Card:

1. Include your contact information, including your social media accounts.

2. Consider a title or branding statement, such as "Writer", "Team Facilitator", or "Volunteer Helping Our Community Thrive", etc.

3. You may want to include a photo.

4. You also may want to leave the back of the card blank to allow for you or your network contact so take notes.

Dr. Rita Smith
Grief Share Volunteer
Supporting People on Their Journey Through Grief
XXX-XXX-XXXX
Email Address
Website URL

Your PERSONAL Business Card

Figure 18

"I AM WOMAN"

Roaring Into Our Retirement

Here we are again, Boomer professional women entering into a new life stage and new territory of retirement. However, this time we have a roadmap. At this stage of our lives, while we may have empty nests and see the decades in our crow's feet, we are confident, savvy, and powerful women ready to reinvent our retirement. Our early career years may have been marked by isolation and even competitiveness with other professional women. However, today we have the maturity and perspective to connect into the collective wisdom of our peers. The women interviewed for this book generously shared their trials and triumphs as they stepped into retirement. Their experiences and learning provide us with a shared "GPS" as we journey along our retirement roadmap.

As we move further into our reinvented retirement, it is no longer possible to keep the "genie" of retirement challenges in her bottle. We Are Women, Hear Us Roar, in Numbers Too Big to Ignore!

Three years into my retirement journey and at the completion of this book, I find myself in a place of contentment, as compared to my early experiences with retirement uncertainty and angst. Using the Reinventing Retirement Roadmap and the associated tools, I have created my wonderful reinvented retirement! I am a professor of management at a local university and enjoy every minute of my second career. I have time for my art and volunteer work. I am embracing my sixth decade with a deep inner sense of what makes my heart sing. My wish for each of you is to go roaring into your retirement and to find what makes your heart sing.

APPENDIX 1

BOOMER RETIREMENT
REIMAGINED WORKSHEETS

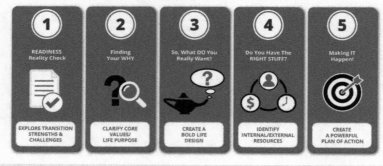

RE-INVENTING BOOMER RETIREMENT: THE ROADMAP

Re-inventing Boomer Retirement
A 5 Step Process for Designing Your Amazing "Second Act"

1	2	3	4	5
READINESS Reality Check	Finding Your WHY	So, What DO You Really Want?	Do You Have The RIGHT STUFF?	Making IT Happen!
EXPLORE TRANSITION STRENGTHS & CHALLENGES	CLARIFY CORE VALUES/ LIFE PURPOSE	CREATE A BOLD LIFE DESIGN	IDENTIFY INTERNAL/EXTERNAL RESOURCES	CREATE A POWERFUL PLAN OF ACTION

Dr. Rita Smith
See Change

RETIREMENT READINESS DIAGNOSTIC QUESTIONNAIRE©

INSTRUCTIONS: Select the response that most accurately describes your level of agreement with the statement. In the blank space to the left of each question, place the number corresponding to your selection. Example:

1. I am confident my retirement will be the best time of my life

1. Strongly Disagree	2. Disagree	3. Agree	4. Strongly Agree
☐	☐	☒	☐

1. I can easily articulate my life purpose.

1. Strongly Disagree	2. Disagree	3. Agree	4. Strongly Agree
☐	☐	☐	☐

2. I share my dreams and fears about retirement with my spouse/partner/significant person.

1. Strongly Disagree	2. Disagree	3. Agree	4. Strongly Agree
☐	☐	☐	☐

3. I spend 5+ hours per month serving my community with my skills and talents.

1. Strongly Disagree	2. Disagree	3. Agree	4. Strongly Agree
☐	☐	☐	☐

4. I am connected to events in our community.

1. Strongly Disagree	2. Disagree	3. Agree	4. Strongly Agree
☐	☐	☐	☐

6. I typically spend 3 + hours per week engaged in hobby activities.

1. Strongly Disagree	2. Disagree	3. Agree	4. Strongly Agree
☐	☐	☐	☐

7. I leverage expert financial retirement advisory resources.

1. Strongly Disagree	2. Disagree	3. Agree	4. Strongly Agree
☐	☐	☐	☐

8. I have multiple non-work opportunities for cognitive enrichment.

1. Strongly Disagree	2. Disagree	3. Agree	4. Strongly Agree
☐	☐	☐	☐

9. I live a majority of life in alignment with my values..

1. Strongly Disagree	2. Disagree	3. Agree	4. Strongly Agree
☐	☐	☐	☐

Dr. Rita Smith

10. I regularly see healthcare professionals for preventative health care.

1. Strongly Disagree	2. Disagree	3. Agree	4. Strongly Agree
☐	☐	☐	☐

11. I am connected with a spiritual community.

1. Strongly Disagree	2. Disagree	3. Agree	4. Strongly Agree
☐	☐	☐	☐

12. I exercise 30 minutes 3-5 times per week.

1. Strongly Disagree	2. Disagree	3. Agree	4. Strongly Agree
☐	☐	☐	☐

13. I have a balanced mix of friends from work and outside of work.

1. Strongly Disagree	2. Disagree	3. Agree	4. Strongly Agree
☐	☐	☐	☐

14. I am satisfied with the amount of leisure time I spend with my family.

1. Strongly Disagree	2. Disagree	3. Agree	4. Strongly Agree
☐	☐	☐	☐

15. I can easily identify new hobbies/leisure activities I will explore in retirement.

1. Strongly Disagree	2. Disagree	3. Agree	4. Strongly Agree
☐	☐	☐	☐

16. I have a diverse network of people in my life.

1. Strongly Disagree	2. Disagree	3. Agree	4. Strongly Agree
☐	☐	☐	☐

17. I am satisfied with my level of physical fitness.

1. Strongly Disagree	2. Disagree	3. Agree	4. Strongly Agree
☐	☐	☐	☐

18. I diligently saved funds for my retirement lifestyle.

1. Strongly Disagree	2. Disagree	3. Agree	4. Strongly Agree
☐	☐	☐	☐

19. I can easily make time for my friends.

1. Strongly Disagree	2. Disagree	3. Agree	4. Strongly Agree
☐	☐	☐	☐

Dr. Rita Smith

20. I regularly seek comfort in spiritual practices during times of uncertainty.

1. Strongly Disagree	2. Disagree	3. Agree	4. Strongly Agree
☐	☐	☐	☐

21. I have a solid plan in place to ensure my retirement aligns with my inner desires.

1. Strongly Disagree	2. Disagree	3. Agree	4. Strongly Agree
☐	☐	☐	☐

22. I can easily identify volunteer activities with which to engage.

1. Strongly Disagree	2. Disagree	3. Agree	4. Strongly Agree
☐	☐	☐	☐

23. I consistently create time and space for my spiritual journey.

1. Strongly Disagree	2. Disagree	3. Agree	4. Strongly Agree
☐	☐	☐	☐

24. I am actively connected to a hobby/leisure community.

1. Strongly Disagree	2. Disagree	3. Agree	4. Strongly Agree
☐	☐	☐	☐

25. I am satisfied with my financial portfolio.

1. Strongly Disagree	2. Disagree	3. Agree	4. Strongly Agree
☐	☐	☐	☐

Dr. Rita Smith

RETIREMENT READINESS DIAGNOSTIC QUESTIONNAIRE©
SCORING

INSTRUCTIONS: Place the numeric score corresponding to each question in the appropriate boxes below. Then total each box. Example:

> **COMMUNITY ENGAGEMENT**
> 3.   2
> 5.   1
> 22. 4
> **Total =**

CLEAR LIFE PURPOSE	COMMUNITY ENGAGEMENT	FAMILY/ RELATIONSHIPS
1. _____	3. _____	2. _____
8. _____	4. _____	13. _____
20. _____	21. _____	18. _____
Total = _____	**Total = _____**	**Total = _____**

FINANCIAL	HOBBY/LEISURE	PHYSICAL HEALTH
6. _____	5. _____	9. _____
17. _____	7. _____	11. _____
23. _____	14. _____	16. _____
Total = _____	**Total = _____**	**Total = _____**

SPIRITUAL DEVELOPMENT	SOCIAL LIFE BEYONDWORK
10. _____	12. _____
19. _____	15. _____
22. _____	21. _____
Total = _____	**Total = _____**

Dr. Rita Smith

WHEEL OF RETIREMENT READINESS©

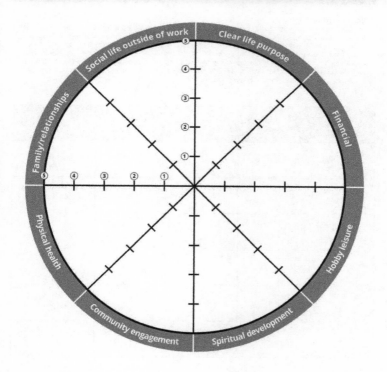

Dr. Rita Smith
Visual Thinking Expert & Transitions Coach
See Change

WORK: POWER & PERKS,
ITS ABOUT MORE THAN JUST THE MONEY©

INSTRUCTIONS:
While it is often easy to list characteristics of work we are happy to leave, such as early alarm clocks and the volume of meetings, it is more difficult to identify what we will lose. In the blank spaces, list what you anticipate losing or have lost due to retirement. Rank the value to you using the ratings Hi, Med. Or Lo. Then, using the same rating scale, rate how difficult it is to replace this loss. Circle your top 3 areas containing both high value and corresponding high difficulty to replace. This reality check about power, perks and other areas of satisfaction gained from work and the difficulty or ease of replacing will be helpful as you create your reinventing retirement plan.

	VALUE	DIFFICULTY TO REPLACE		VALUE	DIFFICULTY TO REPLACE

Dr. Rita Smith
Visual Thinking Expert & Transitions Coach
See Change

TIMELINE OF YOUR LIFE'S KEY TRANSITIONS

Instructions:

In chronological order, reflect upon your key life transitions (going away to college, marriage, new jobs, moving, divorce, etc.). For each key transition decide if this was a difficult/bumpy time for you or a fairly easy, smooth experience. Referring to the vertical continuum of ease and difficulty of transitions, decide where you will place your transition—above or below the line. Briefly identify the transition and approximate date. When complete, review your transitions timeline. What is your first impression? What insights do you have regarding your transitions experiences? How can this insight help you with retirement transition?

Example:

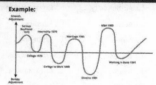

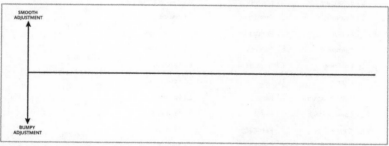

CORE VALUES CHECKLIST©

From the list of core values below, identify your top 20. Once you have checked off your top 20, look at them again. Then highlight, by circling, your top ten. This list is not exhaustive, so feel free to add to it.

☐ Achievement	☐ Determination	☐ Harmony	☐ Purpose
☐ Accountability	☐ Directness	☐ Health	☐ Recognition
☐ Adventure	☐ Drive	☐ Helping others	☐ Religion
☐ Altruism	☐ Duty	☐ Honesty	☐ Resourcefulness
☐ Authenticity	☐ Economic security	☐ Humor	☐ Responsibility
☐ Authority	☐ Education	☐ Imagination	☐ Results
☐ Autonomy	☐ Efficiency	☐ Independence	☐ Risk taking
☐ Balance	☐ Empowerment	☐ Integrity	☐ Routine
☐ Beauty	☐ Environment	☐ Innovation	☐ Security
☐ Belonging	☐ Equality	☐ Intellectual status	☐ Serenity
☐ Boldness	☐ Excellence	☐ Justice	☐ Service
☐ Bravery	☐ Excitement	☐ Knowledge	☐ Sharing
☐ Calmness	☐ Expertise	☐ Leadership	☐ Skill
☐ Challenge	☐ Fairness	☐ Learning	☐ Solitude
☐ Change	☐ Faith	☐ Love	☐ Solving Problems
☐ Collaboration	☐ Fame	☐ Loyalty	☐ Solitude
☐ Commitment	☐ Family	☐ Meaning	☐ Status
☐ Community	☐ Fast Pace	☐ Money	☐ Success
☐ Compassion	☐ Flexibility	☐ Nature	☐ Teaching
☐ Competence	☐ Focus	☐ Openness	☐ Teamwork
☐ Competition	☐ Freedom	☐ Order	☐ Tradition
☐ Conformity	☐ Friendship	☐ Passion	☐ Travel
☐ Creativity	☐ Fun	☐ Peace	☐ Trust
☐ Curiosity	☐ Growth	☐ Power	☐ Variety
☐ Decisiveness	☐ Gratitude	☐ Privacy	☐ Wealth
☐ Dependability	☐ Happiness	☐ Productivity	☐ Winning
			☐ Wisdom

Dr. Rita Smith
See Change

WHAT MAKES YOUR HEART SING?©

The following questions will help you identify what makes your heart sing. Quickly brainstorm what comes up for you from your heart, not your head. Record your list below.

- ✪ What brings you joy?
- ✪ What gets you in a "flow" state, unaware of time and passionately focused?
- ✪ As a child, what did you love to do?
- ✪ When do you feel most alive?

Dr. Rita Smith
Visual Thinking Expert & Transitions Coach
See Change

WHAT ARE YOUR GIFTS TO SHARE WITH THE WORLD?©

What talents and skills do you possess that you want to share with the world?   Write the key words that describe your signature gifts in the arrows below.

WRITING YOUR EULOGY

Imagine you are attending your own funeral. You watch as family and friends step to the podium to make their eulogy to you. They share the way you lived your life and your impact on the world around you. What do you want people to say about you? How do you want to be remembered. Take the time to jot down your thoughts below. It is powerful to see your thoughts in black and white!

_____

_____

_____

_____

_____

_____

_____

To what degree does your current life reflect how you want people to remember you? How can you build yourself in to the person people described?

Dr. Rita Smith
Visual Thinking Expert & Transitions Coach
See Change

RETIREMENT GPS:
CREATING YOUR LIFE PURPOSE STATEMENT©

My life purpose is to use

_____

(my unique talents/qualities)

to_____

(my passion)

_____

_____

So that _____

_____

_____

(meaningful legacy).

Dr. Rita Smith
Visual Thinking Expert & Transitions Coach
See Change

I CAN SEE CLEARLY NOW: DREAM CATCHER©

Catching Your Retirement Dreams: Originating from the Ojibwa (Chippewa) Nation, dream catcher's were believed to alter a person's dreams by protecting the sleeper from negative dreams by catching these bad dreams inside its web. Good dreams filter through the center hole and descend down the feathers to the dreamer. The slightest movement of the feathers would indicate the passage of another beautiful dream. Bad dreams however were trapped in the web and would be burned off by the morning sun.

What retirement dreams do you want to "catch"? Record them in the arrows below.

I CAN SEE CLEARLY NOW: CREATING YOUR VISION BOARD©

WHAT IS A VISION BOARD? A vision board is a goal-setting tool using images and words to clarify your goals, focus your actions, and generate motivation. The process of creating your vision board helps distill what is most important to you and aligned with your values. The very process of selecting pictures engages both reflection and emotion. Science tells us humans are wired to process information visually. Studies of brain neuroplasticity (brain's ability to change) also supports the power of visuals in stimulating neuron activity. From a different perspective, vision boards support the key Law of Attraction tenet, "what you think about, comes about". Vision boards help attract, or manifest, what you want in your life. The bottom line is that focusing and envisioning your goals is a highly effective tool to achieve your retirement vision. Remember you are focusing on the WHAT here, not the HOW.

VISION BOARD EXAMPLE: The vision board pictured below was completed using on-line images. (See Vision Board resource page) Use your creativity. There is no precise formula to create a vision board—there are no rules! Once you have your supplies gathered (See Vision Board checklist page), review your Life Purpose and Values Checklist. Look for images that depict your WHY which will lead you to your WHAT.

PICTURES OF DREAM RETIREMENT   YOUR PHOTO AT CENTER

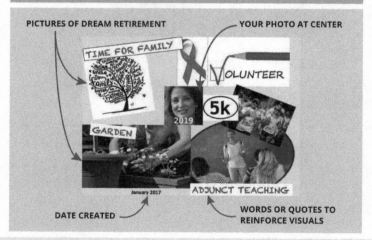

DATE CREATED

WORDS OR QUOTES TO REINFORCE VISUALS

HOW WILL YOU SPEND YOUR NEW FREE TIME?©

2,000 Hours of Free Time: Retirees suddenly find themselves with approximately 2,000 annual hours of free time previously devoted to work. This equates to 7.5 new leisure hours daily [1]. Collectively, over the next two decades, 2.5 trillion leisure hours[2] will be created by retiring Baby Boomers.   After years of structured schedules, leisure time to do with as you wish sounds absolutely wonderful, doesn't it? In practicality, however studies show that over 95%[3] of retirees have no plan for how to maximize this new free time. Studies show traditional retirees spend their time doing the following: approximately 50% of their free time watching television, 30% dedicated to household activities (home improvements, cooking, laundry), 10% eating, and the remaining 10% reading, shopping and socializing.[4] Is this truly the retirement life plan suited to Baby Boomers? How will YOU spend your free time?

In the "pie chart" below, representing 100% of your new, annual leisure time of 2,000 hours, indicate how you will spend your retirement leisure time.

1 U.S. Census Bureau, 2015
2 U.S. Census Bureau, 2016
3 Bureau of Labor Statistics, 2015
4 http://money.usnews.com/money/retirement/articles/2013/07/08/how-retirees-spend-their-time

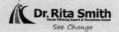

Dr. Rita Smith
Visual Thinking Expert & Transitions Coach
See Change

Conducting a Personal S.W.O.T.: Perhaps you are already familiar with the S.W.O.T. This process is commonly used in organizations to assess themselves as they create and plan to execute on their strategies. S.W.O.T. stands for S= Strengths (internal), W=Weaknesses (internal), O= Opportunities (external) and T = Threats (external).

Used on a personal level, this process captures information about your favorable strengths and what favorable external opportunities and resources are readily available to you. Likewise, your Personal S.W.O.T. assesses areas of weakness such as gaps in required skills or knowledge, time constraints, fears and other internal obstacles and gaps that are barriers in executing your retirement life plan. Finally, it assesses external threats and obstacles, such as limited demand for your area of interest, lack of volunteer roles, potential competition, etc.

Conduct an honest and fearless assessment. Share your Personal S.W.O.T. with people who are candidly able to assess your strengths and weaknesses. Share your assessment with people who have insight into the external opportunities and threats to your retirement life plan . Finally, use your assessment data to inform provide your action plan. Given your S.W.O.T. assessment, what gaps do you need to close?, what threats do you need to mitigate?, what opportunities can you leverage?, what strengths can you leverage and build upon?

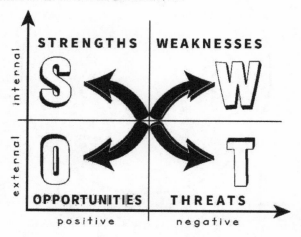

Do You Have the Right Stuff ?: Conducting a Personal S.W.O.T.©

Conducting a Personal S.W.O.T. : To maximize the outcome of this exercise, ensure you have quiet reflection time to complete your Personal S.W.O.T. The questions below are intended to jumpstart your thinking and are certainly not an exhaustive list of inquiries.

Clients report it is helpful to first brainstorm their assessment using sticky notes. This allowed them to combine and/or edit before their final personal assessment was complete.

 Internal Strengths

- What skills do I have that apply to my retirement vision?
- People typically say I am good at _____?
- What personality strengths can I leverage to achieve my retirement life plan?

 Internal Weaknesses

- What skills or knowledge do I need to attain?
- In the past, what has hindered me from achieving goals?
- What am I afraid of?

 External Opportunities

- What education and/or experiences are available for me to close skill or knowledge gaps?
- Who can support me?
- What resources can I tap into to ensure my retirement vision becomes a reality?

 External Threats

- What external obstacles are in my way to success?
- What macro trends could affect my retirement vision?
- What competition exists?

S Internal Strengths	**W** Internal Weaknesses
O External Opportunities	**T** External Threats

Selecting your "Personal Board of Director's " or "Dream Team": First, look beyond your family and close friends who are naturally emotionally invested in you. You want people who will not be biased by their emotional connection with you. Seek people with diverse backgrounds to maximize a variety of perspectives. Be very clear what strengths each person brings to the group and how you plan to leverage these strengths

Name:_____

Key Strength(s):

_____

_____

____

Name:_____

Key Strength(s):

_____

____

Dream Team

Name:_____

Key Strength(s):

_____

____

Name:_____

Key Strength(s):

_____

____

Name:_____

Key Strength(s):

_____

____

Name:_____

Key Strength(s):

_____

____

Do You Have the Right Stuff ?: Mapping My Power Network©

Mapping My Power Network: Networks are relationships that are critical to your ability to learn new skills, access desired opportunities, and advance toward your goal. Being intentional about whom you want in your Power Network is key. In the spaces below, list the names of people you would like to have in your retirement life plan network. Identify network areas requiring further development.

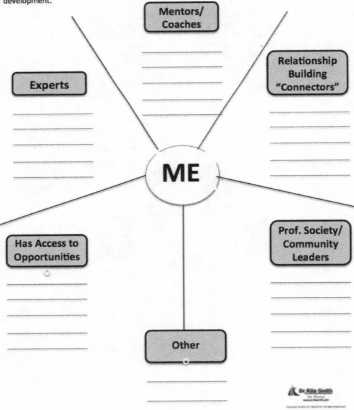

Choosing Your Five Key Action Steps: Review your Closing Gaps © worksheet. From your list of gaps and strategies to close these gaps, what are your top five Big Actions critical to making your Re-Invented Retirement happen? In the spaces below, list the action and target completion date. Identify who will serve as y our accountability partner. From this list you may want to create a more detailed project plan. Please see the Sample Action Plan Timeline on the next page.

MY ACCOUNTABILITY PARTNER:_____

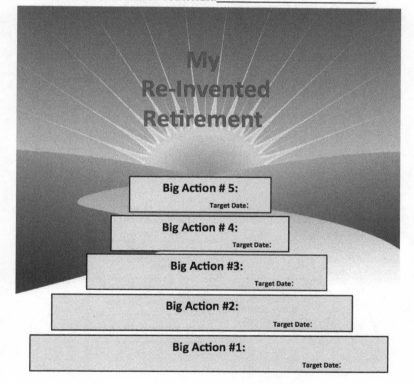

My
Re-Invented
Retirement

Big Action # 5:

Target Date:

Big Action # 4:

Target Date:

Big Action #3:

Target Date:

Big Action #2:

Target Date:

Big Action #1:

Target Date:

Key things to consider when creating your PERSONAL "Business" Card:

1. Include your contact information, including your social media accounts.

2. Consider a title or branding statement, such as "Writer", "Team Facilitator", or "Volunteer Helping Our Community Thrive", etc.

3. You may want to include a photo.

4. You also may want to leave the back of the card blank to allow for you or your network contact so take notes.

Dr. Rita Smith

Grief Share Volunteer
Supporting People on Their Journey Through Grief

XXX-XXX-XXXX
Email Address
Website URL

HEARD IT THROUGH THE GRAPEVINE

Website Resources for Boomer Professional Women

I have collected the following website resources from clients, the amazing women I interviewed, and from my own personal exploration. Each website was screened to ensure its relevancy to our retirement journey. I hope you find these a good starting place. The list is not exhaustive and I am confident your own web surfing will uncover additional relevant resources.

General

1. AARP
AARP.org is the nation's largest nonprofit, nonpartisan organization dedicated to empowering Americans fifty and older to choose how they live as they age.

2. Baby Boomster
Babyboomster.com is a blog dedicated to women midlife and beyond who want to enjoy life on every level

3. Huffington Post Fifty

huffingtonpost.com/fifty offers news, features and the best blogs on topics that matter most to people over fifty.

4. National Association of Baby Boomer Women

nabbw.com/ offers resources for women to explore and empower their passions at midlife.

5. Next Avenue

Nextavenue.org is a digital platform launched by PBS that offers original and aggregated journalism aimed at baby boomers.

Retirement Transition

6. American Psychological Association

Apa.org/search.aspx?query=retirement contains articles and research on the psychological issues of retirement.

7. Boomer Women Speak

Boomerwomenspeak.com is a place for baby boomer women to encourage, connect with, and support one another online.

8. Retire Wow

Retirewow.com provides information and support to help you successfully make the transition from paid work to what's next

9. Retirementally Challenged

Retirementallychallenged.com shares women's insight on learning to navigate their post-work worlds.

10. Second Lives Club

Secondlivesclub.blogspot.com taps into women "making their next life their best life." Focus is on accomplished and professional women reinventing themselves in retirement.

11. The Transition Network

thetransitionnetwork.org is a community of professional women, fifty and forward, whose changing life situations lead them to seek new connections, resources, and opportunities.

Working In Retirement

12. Fab Job

Fabjob.com offers resources to discover and obtain your dream job. Good assortment of e-books on dream jobs.

13. Reboot You

Rebootyou.com is designed to help people reinvent themselves. The site contains resources, examples, stories, inspiration, and information to help you make a transition to your next career. A major focus on retirees but other populations included as well.

14. Retired Brains

Retiredbrains.com is a comprehensive, independent resource website for baby boomers, those planning their retirements, and active retirees.

15. Retire Workforce

Retireeworkforce.com showcases part-time, flexible, and seasonal jobs.

16. SCORE

Score.org is a source of quality free, confidential business education and mentoring. Good resource to support your launching a business.

17. Work Force 50

Workforce50.com has jobs and information to navigate a job search. Topics covered include finding your life's purpose, avoiding mistakes on LinkedIn, and strategic résumé writing.

Volunteering

18. Encore

Encore.org is a non-profit organization dedicated to making it easier for millions of people to pursue encore careers – or second acts for the greater good. Encore encompasses both volunteering and paid work with a focus on purpose.

19. Executive Services Corp

Execservicecorps.org is a United States national network of organizations that provide consulting, coaching, facilitation, and many other **services** to strengthen nonprofits, schools, and government organizations.

20. LinkedIn Volunteer

Linkedinforgood.linkedin.com is a volunteer marketplace that provides volunteer and board opportunities.

21. Oasis Life Long Adventure

Oasisnet.org/National-Programs/Intergenerational-Tutoring provides resources on healthy living, lifelong learning, and volunteer tutoring to enhance students' reading skills.

22. Volunteer Match

Volunteermatch.org brings volunteers and non-profit causes together. Site provides list of opportunities in your area.

Leisure

23. Center for Creative Aging

Creativeaging.org/programs-people/cad provides a searchable tool to identify creative arts education and programs across the US.

24. GVI Travel

Gviusa.com/about-us/why-gvi runs multiple-award-winning, high-quality, and high-impact conservation and community development programs worldwide.

25. Road Scholar

Roadscholar.org is a non-profit organization providing transformational educational adventures.

26. Silver Sneakers

Silversneakers.com is a fitness program provided at no cost to Boomers and beyond, by more than sixty health plans nationwide..

27. Sixty + Me

Sixtyandme.com/list-of-hobbies-for-women-over-50-amazing-ideas-from-the-sixty-and-me-community is a lifestyle resource for Boomer women retirees. It features a robust list of over 42,000 possible leisure activities gathered from from retired Boomer women across the globe.

28. The Women's Travel Group

Thewomenstravelgroup.com provides women age 40+ tours, using smart itineraries, which avoid tourist traps and bus tour restaurants. The tours connect travelers with thought-provoking speakers and insightful experiences.

29. University Based Retirement Communities

bestguide-retirementcommunities.com/Collegelinkedretirementcommunities.html contains a list of US University Based Retirement Communities by region.

NOTES

1 Pascale, R., Primavera, L. H., & Roach, R. (2013). *The retirement maze: what you should know before and after you retire*. Lanham, MD: Rowman & Littlefield. p.

2 Pascale, R., Primavera, L. H., & Roach, R. (2013). *The retirement maze: what you should know before and after you retire*. Lanham, MD: Rowman & Littlefield. p.

3 Pascale, R., Primavera, L. H., & Roach, R. (2013). *The retirement maze: what you should know before and after you retire*. Lanham, MD: Rowman & Littlefield. p.

4 Treen, D. (2009). *Psychology of executive retirement from fear to passion: escape the rat race & save your life*. New York: IUniverse. P.

5 Transamerica. (2016). *17th annusal survey perspectives on retirement: baby boomer, generation x, and millenials*(Rep. No. 17). P. 40

6 Transamerica. (2016). *17th annusal survey perspectives on retirement: baby boomer, generation x, and millenials*(Rep. No. 17). P. 40

7 History.com Staff. (2010). Baby Boomers. Retrieved October 21, 2017, from http://www.history.com/topics/baby-boomers. p.

8 History.com Staff. (2010). Baby Boomers. Retrieved October 21, 2017, from http://www.history.com/topics/baby-boomers. p.

9 History.com Staff. (2010). Baby Boomers. Retrieved October 21, 2017, from http://www.history.com/topics/baby-boomers. p.

10 History.com Staff. (2010). Baby Boomers. Retrieved October 21, 2017, from http://www.history.com/topics/baby-boomers. p.

11 History.com Staff. (2010). Baby Boomers. Retrieved October 21, 2017, from http://www.history.com/topics/baby-boomers. p.

12 History.com Staff. (2010). Baby Boomers. Retrieved October 21, 2017, from http://www.history.com/topics/baby-boomers. p.

13 History.com Staff. (2010). Baby Boomers. Retrieved October 21, 2017, from http://www.history.com/topics/baby-boomers. p.

14 Social Security. (n.d.). Retrieved October 21, 2017, from https://www.ssa.gov/history/age65.html. p.

15 Social Security. (n.d.). Retrieved October 21, 2017, from https://www.ssa.gov/history/age65.html. p.

16 CDC Media Relations: MMWR News Synopsis for July 30, 1999. (n.d.). Retrieved October 21, 2017, from https://www.cdc.gov/media/mmwrnews/1999/n990730.html. p.

17 Ryan, M. P. (2009). *Mysteries of sex: tracing women and men through American history*. Chapel Hill: University of North Carolina Press. p. 231

18 Del webb [Advertisement]. (n.d.).

19 Brandon, Emily. How Retirees Spend Their Time | Retirement | US News. (July 07, 2013) from https://www.money.usnes.com/money/retirement/articles/2013/07/08/how-reitrees-spend-their-time. p.

20 Shifts in Viewing: The Cross-Platform Report Q2 2014. (n.d.). Retrieved October 21, 2017, from http://www.nielsen.com/us/en/insights/reports/2014/shifts-in-viewing-the-cross-platform-report-q2-2014.html. p.

21 Bank of america advisors services. (2014, November 10). How will you spend your 'longevity bonus'. p.

22 Purcell, P. J. (2000). Older workers: employment and retirement trends. *Monthly Labor Review*. P. 24

23 Bankers Life: *New Expectations, New Rewards Work in Retirement for Middle Income Americans* (Rep.). (2015, May). p. 5

24 Bankers Life: *New Expectations, New Rewards Work in Retirement for Middle Income Americans* (Rep.). (2015, May). p. 8

25 Bankers Life: *New Expectations, New Rewards Work in Retirement for Middle Income Americans* (Rep.). (2015, May). p. 13

26 Bankers Life: *New Expectations, New Rewards Work in Retirement for Middle Income Americans* (Rep.). (2015, May). p. 15

27 Bankers Life: *New Expectations, New Rewards Work in Retirement for Middle Income Americans* (Rep.). (2015, May). p.19

28 Kennedy, L. (n.d.). Baby Boomers Open Door to New Housing Options. 21, 2017 http://www.agelessons.com. p.

29 Farrell, D. (2008). *Talkin Bout My Generation: the economic impact of aging baby boomers* (p. 27, Rep.). Mckinesy global Institute. p.10

30 Farrell, D. (2008). *Talkin Bout My Generation: the economic impact of aging baby boomers* (p. 27, Rep.). Mckinesy Global Institute. p.11

31 Farnham, A. (Writer). (2010, December 27) Abc news.

31 Bortz, D. (2012, April 13). Boomer flock to niche retirement communities. http://money.usnews.com/money/retirement/articles/2012/04/13/boomers-flock-to-niche-retirement-communities.

32 Colony, B. S. (n.d.). Burbank Senior Artist Colony. http://www.seniorartistscolony.com/.

33 Keenan, T. (n.d.). *Home and Community Preferences of the 45 Population* (Rep.). GfK Custom Research North America. p. 2

34 Sollisch, J. (2014, November 20). Kicking the Bucket List. *The Washington Post.* http://www.highbeam.com/doc/1P2-37415797.html?refid=easy_hf.p

35 Sabi, *The Boomer Report 2015 An Annual Report of the Baby Boomer Generation* (Rep.). (2015). p.

36 Howe, N. & Strauss, W. (1992, September 30), *Generations: History of America's Future.* Quill, Fort Mill, SC. p.

37 History.com Staff. (2010). Baby Boomers. http://www.history.com/topics/baby-boomers.

38 Peltz, J.. (1988, June 21). It Started With Levittown in 1947 : Nation's 1st Planned Community Transformed Suburbia. http://articles.latimes.com/1988-06-21/business/fi-4744_1_levittown-house.

39 Maier, T. (2003). *Dr. Spock: an American life.* New York: Basic Books. p. 462

40 DeBiasi, C. (n.d.). Television in the 1960's. https://www.sutori.com/story/television-in-the-1960-s-22b16c44-97fd-4f7a-a030-b25159b56015

41 Kline, S.(1993). *Out of the garden: toys, TV and childrens culture in the age of marketing*. Toronto: Garamond Press. p.147.

42 Simon, K.A. & Grant, W.V. (1965). *Digest of Educational Statistics,* Office of Education, Bulletin 1965, No. 4, US Government Printing Office, Washington, D.C. p. 8

43 *School Enrollment-Social and Economic Characteristics of Student: October 1988 and 1987*(P-20, Rep. No. 443). (n.d.). Current Population Reports. Pg. 3

44 Steinberg, C. (1980). *TV facts*. New York, NY: Facts on File. p. 141

45 Steinberg, C. (1980). *TV facts*. New York, NY: Facts on File. p. 141

46 Steinberg, C. (1980). *TV facts*. New York, NY: Facts on File. p. 141

47 Editors of Time-Life Books. (1998), *Rock & Roll Generation, Teen Life in the 50's (Our American Century)*. Time-Life Books, Alexandria, VA. p. 25

48 Joni Mitchell. (1970). *Woodstock* [Vinyl recording]. Atlantic Recording Corp.

49 Influence of the Baby Boomer Generation. (2015, April 17). *Baby Boomer Magazine.com*.

50 Man of the Year. (1967, January 6). *Time*.

51 Croker, R. (2007) *The Boomer Century, 1946-2046 : How america's most influential generation changed everything,* New York: Springboard. p. 57

52 Gillon, S. M. (2004). *Boomer nation: the largest and richest generation ever and how it changed America.* New York: Free Press. p. 33.

53 Chicago/we can change the world [Recorded by G. Nash]. (1971). On *Chicago*[Vinyl recording]. Atlantic.

54 Sheehy, G. (1974). *Passages: predictable crises of adult life.* New York: Dutton. p. 37

55 Cohen, P. (2013). *In our prime: the fascinating history and promising future of middle age.* New York: Scribner. p. 4.

56 Burghardt, L. (2002). *The happy empty nest: rediscovering love and success after your kids leave home.* New York, NY: Kensington Pub. p. 33

57 Oliver, R. (1982). "Empty Nest" or Relationship Restructuring? *Women & Therapy,1*(2), 67-83. p. 67.

58 Borland, D.C. (1982). A Cohort Analysis Approach to the Empty-Nest Syndrome among Three Ethnic Groups of Women: A Theoretical Position. *Journal of Marriage and the Family,44*(1), 117. p. 117.

59 Rubenstein, C. (2007). *Beyond the mommy years: how to live happily ever after-- after the kids leave home.* New York: Springboard Press. p. 15.

60 Raup, J. L., & Myers, J. E. (1989). The Empty Nest Syndrome: Myth or Reality? *Journal of Counseling & Development,68*(2), 180-183. p. 181.

61 Pope, A. (2005). Personal Transformation in Midlife Orphanhood: An Empirical Phenomenological Study. *OMEGA - Journal of Death and Dying,51*(2), 107-123. p. 108.

62 Scott, P. S. (2017, October 04). 6 Reasons a Parent's Death Is a Special Kind of Loss. https://www.caring.com/articles/death-of-a-parent.

63 "The Last Goodbye: When both parents die, middle-aged children must adjust to a new stage of life in which they become adult orphans", *TIME*, November 13, 2000. http://content.time.com/time/magazine/article/0,9171,59796,00.html.

64 "The Last Goodbye: When both parents die, middle-aged children must adjust to a new stage of life in which they become adult orphans", *TIME*, November 13, 2000. http://content.time.com/time/magazine/article/0,9171,59796,00.html.

65sixty-five Gonyea, J. G. (1998). *Midlife and Menopause: Uncharted Territories for Baby Boomer Women,* 22 (1) Spring. p. 87.

66 Kearney, L. (2017, March 15). US plastic surgery, cosmetic spending hits record $15 billion. https://www.reuters.com/article/us-usa-plasticsurgery/u-s-plastic-surgery-cosmetic-spending-hits-record-15-billion-idUSKBN16M3B1.

67 Goff Goldberg, K. (2009, February 25). *Gray hair is not always something to dye for* http://www.washingtontimes.com/news/2009/feb/25/gray-hair-not-always-something-to-dye-for/

68 Joni Mitchell. (1970). *Woodstock* [Vinyl recording]. Atlantic Recording Corp.

69 Park, A. (2015, July 25). Menopause Accelerates Aging in Women. (http://time.com/4422860/menopause-accelerates-aging/.

70 International Labor Office, (2016). http://www.ilo.org/global/research/global-reports/weso/2016/WCMS_443480/lang--en/index.html.

71 https://www.starbucks.com/about-us/company-information/mission-statement.

72 Lauricella, Tom. (2014, November 1). For Some, Retirement Brings Grief. Wall Street Journal

73 Jungmeen, E. and Moen, P. (2002) *Retirement Transitions, Gender, and Psychological Well-Being: A Life-Course, Ecological Model*

The Journals of Gerontology: Series B, Volume 57, Issue 3, 1 May 2002, Pages p. 212–222, p. 216.

74 Loe, M. and Johnston, D. K. (2016, May 4). *Professional Women "Rebalancing" Time, Relationships, and Body.* Women and Aging, Volume 28 2016, Issue 5, P418-430. p. 423

75 Holmes, T. H., & Rahe, R. H. (1967) *"Social Readjustment Rating Scale."* Journal of Psychosom Res 11 (2). Pages 213-128, pg. 214.

76 Bridges, W. (2009). *Transitions: making sense of lifes changes.* Cambridge, MA: Da Capo Press. p. 33.

77 (Bridges, p. 122)

78 Atchley. (2015, May). The 6 Stages of Retirement. Re-trieved November 05, 2017, from http://retirementjour-neys.com/2015/07/the-6-stages-of-retirement/

79 (Atchley, 2015)

80 Chamberlain, J. (2014) *Retiring minds want to know* **What's the key to a smooth retirement? Tend to your psychological portfolio as much as your financial one, re-searchers say.** APA Monitor on Psychology. (45), 1. p. 61.

81 Mass mutual. (2015). *Parellel Lives: How men and Wom-en Experience Retirement Differently.*(Rep.). https://www.massmutual.com/about-us/news-and-press-releases/press-releases/2015/06/03/11/15/parallel-lives-how-men-and-women-experience-retirement-differently.

82 Rich, P., Sampson, D. M., & Fetherling, D. (2000). *The healing journey through retirement: your journal of transi-tion and transformation.* New York: John Wiley. P. 54

83 (APA Monitor on Psychology. (45), 1. p. 61.)

84 (Bridges, p. 122)

85 Hill, P. L., & Turiano, N. A. (2014). *Purpose in Life as a Predictor of Mortality Across Adulthood*. Psychological Science,25 (7), 1482-1486. p. 1484.

86 (Age Wave and Merrill Lynch. (2014). *Health and retirement: planning for the great unknown.* http://agewave. com/wp-content/uploads/2016/07/2014-ML-AW-Health-and-Retirement_Planning-for-the-Great-Unknown.pdf

87 AARP. (May 2004.). *"The Divorce Experience: A Study of Divorce at Midlife and Beyond"* (Rep.).

88 Valeo, T. (Jan 9, 2006.). Baby Boomers: A New Way to Grow Old. Retrieved November 05, 2017, from https:// www.webmd.com/healthy-aging/features/baby-boomers-and-retirement#1

89 Michelle C. Carlson, Kirk I. Erickson, Arthur F. Kramer, Michelle W. Voss, Natalie Bolea, Michelle Mielke, Sylvia McGill, George W. Rebok, Teresa Seeman, Linda P. Fried; Evidence for Neurocognitive Plasticity in At-Risk Older Adults: The Experience Corps Program, *The Journals of Gerontology: Series A*, Volume 64A, Issue 12, 1 December 2009, Pages 1275–1282, p. 1280. https://doi.org/10.1093/gerona/glp117

90 Moore, S. C., Patel, A. V., Matthews, C. E., Gonzalez, A. B., Park, Y., Katki, H. A., . . . Lee, I. (2012). Leisure Time Physical Activity of Moderate to Vigorous Intensity and Mortality: A Large Pooled Cohort Analysis. *PLoS Medicine,9* (11). doi:10.1371/journal.pmed.1001335

91 Vernon. (2017). *Life Planning in the age of longevity.* Stanford Center on Longevity (Rep.). p. 4.

92 Argyris, C. (2015). Double-Loop Learning. *Wiley Encyclopedia of Management,*1-2. doi:10.1002/9781118785317. weom110140. p. 1.

93 DRUCKER, P. F. (2010). *CHANGING WORLD OF THE EXECUTIVE.* Harvard Business School Press, Boston , MA. p. 87.

94 Erikson, E. H., Erikson, J. M., & Kivnick, H. Q. (1994). *Vital involvement in old age.* New York: Norton. p. 241.

95 Leider, R. (2015). *The Power and Purpose: Find Meaning, Live longer, Better* (3rd ed.). Oakland, CA: Berrett-Kohler. p. 33.

96 (Leider, pg. 36).

97 Dan Buettner (September 2009). *How to live to be 100+,* TED Talk,

98 Koizumi, M., Ito, H., Kaneko, Y., & Motohashi, Y. (2008). Effect of Having a Sense of Purpose in Life on the Risk of Death from Cardiovascular Diseases. *Journal of Epidemiology,18*(5), 191-196. p. 192. doi:10.2188/jea.je2007388

99 Boyle, P. A., Buchman, A. S., Barnes, L. L., & Bennett, D. A. (2010). Effect of a Purpose in Life on Risk of Incident Alzheimer Disease and Mild Cognitive Impairment in Community-Dwelling Older Persons. *Archives of General Psychiatry,67*(3), 304-310. p. 307. doi:10.1001/archgenpsychiatry.2009.208

100 Leider, R. (2009). *Discovering what matters: balancing money, medicine, and meaning.*(Rep.). Westport, CT: Metlife Mature Market Institute. p. 8.

101 (Leider, 2009, p. 9).

102 (Leider, 2009, p. 14).

103 Nelson, J. E., & Bolles, R. N. (2010). *What color is your parachute? for retirement: planning a prosperous, healthy, and happy future.* Berkeley: Ten Speed Press. p. 5.

104 Csikszentmihalyi, M. (2009). *Flow: The psychology of optimal experience.* New York: Harper Row. p. 67-72.

105 Robinson, K., & Aronica, L. (2013). *Finding your element: how to discover your talents and passions and transform your life.* New York: Viking. p. 33.

106 (Leider, 2009, p. 37).

107 (Leider, 2009, p. 40)

108 Burnett, W., & Evans, D. J. (2017). *Designing your life: how to build a well-lived, joyful life.* New York: Alfred A. Knopf. p. xvi.

109 (Burnett & Evans, 2017, p. 68).

110 Dream Catcher History & Legend. (n.d.). Retrieved November 05, 2017, from http://www.dream-catchers.org/

111 Turner, M. L. (2010). *The complete idiots guide to vision boards.* Indianapolis, IN: Alpha Books. p. 4.

112 How to Cultivate Your Creativity [Book Excerpt ... (January 1, 2016). Retrieved November 5, 2017, from https://www.bing.com/cr?IG=CF439BA3AD4844D4B3E63F22EFABF6ED&CID=274A903B0F346419329F9B0A0E326533&rd=1&h=dBdeSxjaVaCFEJBngyxuowwawIlBPwt7malkGaW8dQ8&v=1&r=https%3a%2f%2fwww.scientificamerican.com%2farticle%2fhow-to-cultivate-your-creativity-book-excerpt%2f&p=DevEx,5068.1

113 Sprenger, M. (2010). *The leadership brain for dummies.* Hoboken, NJ: Wiley Pub. p. 21.

REFERENCES

1.https://www.money.usnews.com/money/retirement/ articles/2012/04/13/boomers-flock-to-niche-retirement-communities

2. https://www.sutori.com/story/television-in-the-1960-s-22b16c44-97fd-4f7a-a030-b25159b56015

3. http://www.ilo.org/global/research/global-reports/we-so/2016/WCMS_443480/lang--en/index.html

4. (Rep.). (n.d.). Mass Mutual.

5. https ://agewave.com/wp-content/uploads/2016/07/2014-ML-AW-Health-and-Retirement_Planning-for-the-Great-Un-known.pdf

6. https://www.jhsph.edu/news/news-releases/2009/carl-son-brain-scan.html

7. https://www.apa.org/monitor/2014/01/retiring-minds.aspx

8. *2016 International Labor Office Report* (Rep.). (2016).

9. AARP. (n.d.). *On women initiating divorce* (Rep.).

10. AARP. (n.d.). *"The Divorce Experience: A Study of Divorce at Midlife and Beyond"* (Rep.).

11. Age Wave and Merrill Lynch. (2014). *Health and retirement: planning for the great unknown*.

12. Altshuler, G. (2003). All Shook Up: How Rock 'n' Roll Changed America (Pivotal Moments in American History). Oxford Press, New York, NY.

13. Argyris, C. (2015). Double-Loop Learning. *Wiley Encyclopedia of Management,* 1-2.

14. Atchley. (2015, May). The 6 Stages of Retirement. http://retirementjourneys.com/2015/07/the-6-stages-of-retirement/

15. Bank of America Advisors Services. (2014, November 10). How will you spend your "longevity bonus."

16. Attwood, J. B., & Attwood, C. (2009). *The passion test: the effortless path to discovering your destiny*. London: Pocket.

17. Bannon, B., Chemers, A., & Thralls, M. (2012). *The Empty Desk Survival Guide: for women on the verge of retirement or encore careers*. Charleston, SC: CreateSpace.

17. Borland, D. C. (1982). A Cohort Analysis Approach to the Empty-Nest Syndrome among Three Ethnic Groups of Women: A Theoretical Position. *Journal of Marriage and the Family, 44*(1), 117.

18. Bortz, D. (n.d.). Boomer flock to niche retirement communities. http://money.usnews.com/money/retirement/articles/2012/04/13/boomers-flock-to-niche-retirement-communities

19. Boyle, P. A., Buchman, A. S., Barnes, L. L., & Bennett, D. A. (2010). Effect of a Purpose in Life on Risk of Incident Alzheimer Disease and Mild Cognitive Impairment in Community-Dwelling Older Persons. *Archives of General Psychiatry, 67*(3), 304.

20. Bovey, S. (1995). *The empty nest: when children leave home*. London: Pandora.

21. Bradford, L. P., & Bradford, M. I. (1979). *Retirement: coping with emotional upheavals*. Chicago: Nelson-Hall.

22. Brandon, E. (2013, July 8). How Retirees Spend Their Time | Retirement | US News. Retrieved October 21, 2017, from https://www.bing.com/cr?IG=C94A339C788B4529A7EC4963542BC3CF&CID=0D189632808069A82DED9D10818668E0&rd=1&h=G0i60oDPcttjGMoGfUZZrBB4PGqjvhhJJtM6gRzl8lU&v=1&r=https%3a%2f%2fmoney.usnews.com%2fmoney%2fretirement%2farticles%2f2013%2f07%2f08%2fhow-retirees-spend-their-time&p=DevEx,5069.1

23. Bratter, B. (2013). *Project renewment: the first retirement model for career women*. Scribner.

24. Bridges, W. (2009). *Transitions: making sense of lifes changes*. Cambridge, MA: Da Capo Press.

25. Bronfman, E. M., & Whitney, C. (2002). *The third act: reinventing yourself after retirement*. New York: G.P. Putman.

26. Buckingham, M., & Clifton, D. O. (2005). *Now, discover your strengths: how to develop your talents and those of the people you manage*. London: Pocket Books.

27. Buettner, D. (2014.). *How to live to be 100*. TED Talk. https://tedsummaries.com/2014/11/04/dan-buettner-how-to-live-to-be-100/

28. Burghardt, L. (2002). *The happy empty nest: rediscovering love and success after your kids leave home*. New York, NY: Kensington Pub.

29. Burnett, W., & Evans, D. J. (2017). *Designing your life: how to build a well-lived, joyful life*. New York: Alfred A. Knopf.

30. Cantor, D. W., & Thompson, A. (2002). *What do you want to do when you grow up?: starting the next chapter of your life*. Boston: Little, Brown.

31. Carlson. (2009). *For older adults; participating in social service activities can improve brain function* (Rep.).

32. Carlson, M. C., Erickson, K. I., Kramer, A. F., Voss, M. W., Bolea, N., Mielke, M., Fried, L. P. (2009, August 19). Evidence for Neurocognitive Plasticity in At-Risk Older Adults: The Experience Corps Program | The Journals of Gerontology: Series A | Oxford Academic. https://academic.oup.

com/biomedgerontology/article/64A/12/1275/566878/Ev-
idence-for-Neurocognitive-Plasticity-in-At-Risk?maxtoshow
=&HITS=10&hits=10&RESULTFORMAT=&fulltext=volunteer
ing&searchid=1&FIRSTINDEX=0&resourcetype=HWCIT

33. CDC Media Relations: MMWR News Synopsis for July
30, 1999. https://www.cdc.gov/media/mmwrnews/1999/
n990730.htm

34. Cohen, P. (2013). *In our prime: the fascinating history
and promising future of middle age*. New York: Scribner.

35. Collins, G. (2014). *When everything changed: the amazing journey of American women from 1960 to the present:
a keepsake journal*. New York: Little, Brown and Company.

36. Colony, B. S. (n.d.). Burbank Senior Artist Colony. http://
www.seniorartistscolony.com/

37. Croker, R. (2007). *The Boomer Century, 1946-2046: How
America's Most Influential Generation Changed Everything.*
Springboard Press, New York, NY.

38. Csikszentmihalyi, M. (2009). *Flow: The psychology of optimal experience*. New York: Harper Row.

39. Dailey, N. (2000). *When baby boom women retire*. Westport, CT: Praeger.

40. Delamontagne, R. P. (2010). *The retiring mind: how to
make the psychological transition to retirement*. Place of
publication not identified: Fairview Imprints.

41. Del webb [Advertisement]. (n.d.).

42. Douglas, S. J. (1995). *Where the girls are: growing up female with the mass media*. New York: Times Books.

43. Dream Catcher History & Legend. (n.d.). http://www.dream-catchers.org/

44. DRUCKER, P. F. (2016). *CHANGING WORLD OF THE EXECUTIVE*. Place of publication not identified: TAYLOR & FRANCIS.

45. Duckworth, C., & Langworthy, M. (2013). *Shifting gears to your life & work after retirement*. Sherrills Ford, NC: New Cabady Press.

46. Erikson, E. H. (1980). *Identity and the life cycle*. New York: Norton.

47. Erikson, E. H., Erikson, J. M., & Kivnick, H. Q. (1994). *Vital involvement in old age*. New York: Norton.

48. Erickson, T. J. (2008). *Retire retirement: career strategies for the boomer generation*. Boston, MA: Harvard Business School Press.

49. Evans, S. B., & Avis, J. P. (1999). *The women who broke all the rules*. Naperville, IL: Sourcebooks.

50. Evans, S. M. (2004). Tidal Wave: How Women Changed America at Century's End Reprint Edition. Free Press, New York, NY.

51. Farnham, A. (Writer). (n.d.). Abc news [Television series episode]. In *ABC news*.

52. Farrell, C. (2016). *Unretirement: how baby boomers are changing the way we think about work, community, and the good life*. New York: Bloomsbury Press.

53. Farrell, D. (2008). *Talkin Bout My Generation: the economic impact of aging baby boomers* (p. 27, Rep.). Mckinesy global Institute.

54. Ford, D. (2012). *The dark side of the light chasers reclaiming your power, creativity, brilliance, and dreams*. Carlsbad, CA: Hay House Audio.

55. Freedman, M. (2008). *Encore: Finding Work that Matters in the Second Half of Life*. PublicAffairs.

56. Freedman, M. (2011). *The big shift: navigating the new stage beyond midlife*. New York: PublicAffairs.

57. Froehlich, M. A. (2005). *When you're facing the empty nest*. Minneapolis, MN: Bethany House .

58. Funderburg, L. (00, November 13). The last goodbye: when both parents die, middle-aged children must adjust to a new stage of life in which they become adult orphans. *Time*.

59. Gillon, S. M. (2004). *Boomer nation: the largest and richest generation ever and how it changed America*. New York: Free Press.

60. Gourley, C. (2008). *Ms. and the material girls: perceptions of women from the 1970s through the 1990s*. Minneapolis, MN: Twenty-First Century Books.

61. *Health and retirement: planning for the great unknown* (Rep.). (n.d.).

62. Hill, P. L., & Turiano, N. A. (2014). Purpose in Life as a Predictor of Mortality Across Adulthood. *Psychological Science, 25*(7), 1482-1486.

63. Hine, T. (2000). *The rise and fall of the American teenager*. New York: Perennial.

64. History.com Staff. (2010). Baby Boomers. http://www.history.com/topics/baby-boomers

sixty-five. Holmes, T. H., & Rahe, R. H. (n.d.). Social Readjustment Rating Scale. *PsycTESTS Dataset*.

66. How Retirees Spend Their Time | Retirement | US News. (n.d.). https://www.money.usnes.com/money/retirement/articles/2013/07/08/how-reitrees-spend-their-time

67. How to Cultivate Your Creativity [Book Excerpt ... (n.d.). https://www.bing.com/cr?IG=CF439BA3AD4844D4B3E63F 22EFABF6ED&CID=274A903B0F346419329F9B0A0E32653 3&rd=1&h=dBdeSxjaVaCFEJBngyxuowwawIlBPwt7malkGa W8dQ8&v=1&r=https%3a%2f%2fwww.scientificamerican. com%2farticle%2fhow-to-cultivate-your-creativity-book-excerpt%2f&p=DevEx,5068.1

68. Howe, N., & Strauss, W. (1992). *Generations: History of America's Future.* Fort mill, SC.

69. *Http://www.ilo.org/global/research/global-reports/we-so/2016/WCMS_443480/lang--en/index.htm* (Rep.). (n.d.).

70. *Https://www.aarp.org/research/topics/life/info-2014/divorce.html* (Rep.). (n.d.). doi:https://www.aarp.org/re-search/topics/life/info-2014/divorce.html

71. Influence of the Baby Boomer Generation. (2015, April 17). *Baby Boomer Magazine.com.*

72. Jenkins, P. (2009). *What will I do all day?: wisdom to get over retirement and on with living!* United States?: P. Jenkins.

73. Kearney, L. (2017, March 15). US plastic surgery, cosmetic spending hits record $15 billion. https://www.reuters.com/article/us-usa-plasticsurgery/u-s-plastic-surgery-cos-metic-spending-hits-record-15-billion-idUSKBN16M3B1

74. Keenan, T. (n.d.). *Home and Community Preferences of the 45 Population* (Rep.). GfK Custom Research North America.

75. Kennedy, L. (n.d.). Baby Boomers Open Door to New Housing Options. http://www.agelessons.com

76. Kearney, L. (2017, March 15). US plastic surgery, cosmetic spending hits record $15 billion. https://www.reuters.com/article/us-usa-plasticsurgery/u-s-plastic-surgery-cos-metic-spending-hits-record-15-billion-idUSKBN16M3B1

77. Kline, S. (1993). *Out of the garden: toys, TV and children's culture in the age of marketing*. Toronto: Garamond Press.

78. Koenig, H. G. (2003). *Purpose and power in retirement: new opportunities for meaning and significance*. Philadelphia: Templeton Foundation Press.

79. Koizumi, M., Ito, H., Kaneko, Y., & Motohashi, Y. (2008). Effect of Having a Sense of Purpose in Life on the Risk of Death from Cardiovascular Diseases. *Journal of Epidemiology, 18*(5), 191-196. doi:10.2188/jea.je2007388

80. Lawrence-Lightfoot, S. (2010). *The third chapter: passion, risk, and adventure in the 25 years after 50*. New York: Farrar, Straus and Giroux.

81. Leider, R. (2009). *Discovering what matters: balancing money, medicine, and meaning*. (Rep.). Westport, CT: Metlife Mature Market Institute.

82. Leider, R. (2015). *The Power and Purpose: FInd Meaning, Live longer, netter* (3rd ed.). Oakland, CA: Berrett-Kohler.

83. Levine, S. (2006). *Inventing the rest of our lives: women in second adulthood*. New York: Plume.

84. Maglin, N. B., & Radosh, A. (2003). *Women confronting retirement: a nontraditional guide*. New Brunswick, NJ: Rutgers University Press.

85. Maier, T. (2003). *Dr. Spock: an American life*. New York: Basic Books.

86. Man of the Year. (1967, January 6). *Time*.

87. Mass mutual. (2015). *Parellel Lives: How men and Women Experience Retirement Differently* (Rep.).

88. McCarthy, S. C. (2014). *Boomers 101: the definitive collection*. Washington, DC: AARP.

89. McCaw, D. (2011). *Its your time: information and exercises to get you ready for a great retirement*. Toronto: BPS Books.

90. McKenna, E. P. (1998). *When work doesn't work anymore: women, work and identity*. New York, NY: Delta.

91. Menopause Accelerates Aging in Women. (n.d.). http://time.com/4422860/menopause-accelerates-aging/

92. Meilleur, T. (2011). Your next chapter: five steps to creating the life of your dreams. Self –Published.

93. Milne, D. (2013). *The psychology of retirement: coping with the transition from work*. Chichester, West Sussex, U.K.: Wiley-Blackwell.

94. Mitchell, J. (1970). *Woodstock* [Vinyl recording]. Atlantic Recording Corp.

95. Moen, P., & Roehling, P. (2005). *The career mystique: cracks in the American dream*. Lanham: Rowman & Littlefield.

96. Moore, S. C., Patel, A. V., Matthews, C. E., Gonzalez, A. B., Park, Y., Katki, H. A., . . . Lee, I. (2012). Leisure Time Physical Activity of Moderate to Vigorous Intensity and Mortality: A Large Pooled Cohort Analysis. *PLoS Medicine, 9*(11).

97. Nash, G. Chicago/we can change the world [Recorded by G. Nash]. (1971).On *Chicago* [Vinyl recording]. Atlantic.

98. *Neilsen Historical Daily Viewing Activity Among Households & Persons 2* (Rep.). (n.d.).

99. Nelson, J. E., & Bolles, R. N. (2010). *What color is your parachute? for retirement: planning a prosperous, healthy, and happy future.* Berkeley: Ten Speed Press.

100. *New Expectations, New Rewards Work in Retirement for Middle Income Americans* (Rep.). (2015).

101. Newman, B. K. (2008). *Retiring as a career: making the most of your retirement.* Westport, CT: Praeger.

102. Oliver, R. (1982). "Empty Nest" or Relationship Restructuring? *Women & Therapy, 1*(2), 67-83.

103. *Parellel Lives: How en and Women Experience Retirement Differently* (Rep.). (2015).

104. Pascale, R., Primavera, L. H., & Roach, R. (2013). *The retirement maze: what you should know before and after you retire.* Lanham, MD: Rowman & Littlefield.

105. Peltz, J.F., Times Staff Writer. (1988, June 21). It Started With Levittown in 1947 : Nation's 1st Planned Community Transformed Suburbia. http://articles.latimes.com/1988-06-21/business/fi-4744_1_levittown-house

106. Perkins-Reed, M. A. (1996). *Thriving in transition: effective living in times of change.* New York: Simon & Schuster.

107. Pope, A. (2006). *From child to elder: personal transformation in becoming an orphan at midlife.* New York: P. Lang.

108. Pope, A. (2005). Personal Transformation in Midlife Orphanhood: An Empirical Phenomenological Study. *OMEGA - Journal of Death and Dying, 51*(2), 107-123.

109. Purcell, P. J. (2000). Older workers: employment and retirement trends. *Monthly Labor Review.*

110. Raup, J. L., & Myers, J. E. (1989). The Empty Nest Syndrome: Myth or Reality? *Journal of Counseling & Development, 68*(2), 180-183.

111. Rentsch, G. (2008) *Smart women don't retire-they break free.* The Transition Network. Springboard Press, New York, NY.

112. Reynolds, M., & Reynolds, M. (2010). *Wander woman: how high-achieving women find contentment and direction.* San Francisco: Berrett-Koehler.

113. Rich, P., Sampson, D. M., & Fetherling, D. (2000). *The healing journey through retirement: your journal of transition and transformation.* New York: John Wiley.

114. Rimbach, P. K. (2011) Retirement: Life's Mt. Everest, Xlibris, Corp.

115. Robinson, K., & Aronica, L. (2013). *Finding your element: how to discover your talents and passions and transform your life*. New York: Viking.

116. Roche-Tarry, D., & Roche-Lebrec, D. (2012). *Whats next?: how professionals are refusing retirement*. Basingstoke: Palgrave Macmillan.

117. Rockefeller, B., & Tate, N. J. (2014). *Da Vincis baby boomer survival guide: live, prosper, and thrive in your retirement*. Boca Raton, FL: Humanix Books.

118. Rossetti, L. (2015). *Women and transition: reinventing work and life*. Basingstoke, Hampshire: Palgrave Macmillan.

119. Roy, D. (2015). *The essential guide to retirement readiness: finances, health & wellness, relationships, life purpose*. Ottawa, Ontario: Daniel Roy.

120. Rubenstein, C. (2007). *Beyond the mommy years: how to live happily ever after-- after the kids leave home*. New York: Springboard Press.

121. Ryan, M. P. (2009). *Mysteries of sex: tracing women and men through American history*. Chapel Hill: University of North Carolina Press.

122. Sagert, K. B. (2007). *The 1970s*. Westport, CT: Greenwood Press.

123. Sanvidge, S. (2010). *Penny loafers & bobby pins: tales and tips from growing up in the 50s and 60s*. Madison, WI: Wisconsin Historical Society Press.

124. Schlossberg, N. K. (2009). *Retire Smart, Retire Happy: Finding Your True Path in Life*. Washington: American Psychological Association.

125. Schlossberg, N. K. (2009). *Revitalizing retirement: reshaping your identity, relationships, and purpose*. Washington, DC: American Psychological Association.

126. *School Enrollment-Social and Economic Characteristics of Student: October 1988 and 1987* (P-20, Rep. No. 443). (n.d.). Current Population Reports.

127. Schwartz, J. (2010). *The Vision Board The Secret to an Extraordinary Life*. New York, NY: Collins Design.

128. Scott, P. S. (2017, October 04). 6 Reasons a Parent's Death Is a Special Kind of Loss. https://www.caring.com/articles/death-of-a-parent

129. Sedlar, J., & Miners, R. (2003). *Dont retire, rewire!: 5 steps to fulfilling work that fuels your passion, suits your personality, or fills your pocket*. Indianapolis, IN: Alpha.

130. Sheehy, G. (1974). *Passages: predictable crises of adult life*. New York, NY: Dutton.

131. Shellenbarger, S. (2005). *The breaking point: how today's women are navigating midlife crisis*. New York: Henry Holt.

132. Shepard, M. D., Dobb, S., & Crandall, S. (2012). *Preparing for your prime time: a woman boomers guide to retirement*. Place of publication not identified: Xlibris Corp.

133. Shifts in Viewing: The Cross-Platform Report Q2 2014. http://www.nielsen.com/us/en/insights/reports/2014/shifts-in-viewing-the-cross-platform-report-q2-2014.html

134. Shultz, K. S., Kaye, M., & Annesley, M. (2015). *Happy retirement: the psychology of reinvention*. NY, NY: DK.

135. Simon, K. (1965). *Digest of Educational Statistics* (Vol. 4, Rep.).

Social Security. https://www.ssa.gov/history/age65.html

136. Sollisch, J. (2014, November 20). Kicking the bucket list [Web log post].

The Washington Post.

137. Spangler, L. C. (2003). *Television women from Lucy to Friends: fifty years of sitcoms and feminism*. Westport: Praeger.

138. Spector, A., & Lawrence, K. (2010). *Your retirement quest: 10 secrets for creating and living a fulfilling retirement*. Cincinnati, OH: Cincinnati Book.

139. Sprenger, M. (2010). *The leadership brain for dummies*. Hoboken, NJ: Wiley Pub.

140. Steinberg, C. (1980). *TV facts*. New York, NY: Facts on File.

141. Sundstrom, E. D., Burnham, R., & Burnham, M. (2007). *My next phase: the personality-based guide to your best retirement*. New York, NY: Springboard Press.

142. *The Boomer Report Annual Study of Baby Boomer Generation* (Rep.). (2015).

143. *The Bureau of Labor Statistics American Time Use Survey* (Rep.). (2013).

Transamerica. (2016). *17th annual survey perspectives on retirement: baby boomer, generation x, and millenials* (Rep. No. 17).

144. Thomas, P. J. (2013). *Retirement by design: how to pursue your passions, leave your legacy and live the retirement of your dreams*. Diamond Perspectives, Richmond, VA.

145. Treen, D. (2009). *Psychology of executive retirement from fear to passion: escape the rat race & save your life*. New York: IUniverse.

146. Turner, M. L. (2010). *The complete idiots guide to vision boards*. Indianapolis, IN: Alpha Books.

147. Valeo, T. (January 9, 2006.). Baby Boomers: A New Way to Grow Old. https://www.webmd.com/healthy-aging/features/baby-boomers-and-retirement#1

148. Vernon. (2017). *Life Planning in the age of longevity* (Rep.).

149. Weiss, R. S. (2005). *The experience of retirement*. Ithaca, N.Y.: Cornell Univ. Press.

150. Yount, D. (2005). *Celebrating the rest of your life*. Minneapolis, MN: Augsburg.

INDEX

CPSIA information can be obtained
at www.ICGtesting.com
Printed in the USA
LVHW04s2205140518
577211LV00001B/25/P